BOOST YOUR ENERGY

For Women Juggling Home and Work

Eileen Gillibrand
& Jenny Mosley

Foreword by Anita Roddick

Positive Press

Positive Press Ltd
28A Gloucester Road
Trowbridge
Wiltshire BA14 0AA
England

New edition in revised format published by Positive Press, 2001
First published by Thorsons in 1995 under the title *When I Go to Work I Feel Guilty*

ISBN 0 9530122 4 7

Printed in England

Contents

About the authors

Eileen Gillibrand and Jenny Mosley have combined many years working in education, counselling and management training, with motherhood – they each have three children.

Eileen and Jenny teach on a wide range of university and college courses and are currently involved in research into how education could do more to counteract the underachievement and enhance the self-esteem of women of all ages. Both travel across the UK as consultants and trainers to education, industry and the caring services in the areas of promoting self-esteem, developing positive relationships and enhancing quality management skills. Between them they have written twenty books on the above areas. They offer a range of consultancy services for individuals or enlightened establishments concerned to promote personal and professional development of women. They can be contacted as follows:

Eileen Gillibrand
School of Education
Bristol University
35 Berkeley Square
Bristol BS8 1JA
Tel: 0117 928 7023
Fax: 0117 925 1537

Jenny Mosley
The Jenny Mosley Consultancies
28A Gloucester Road
Trowbridge
Wiltshire BA14 0AA
Tel: 01225 767157
Fax: 01225 755631

Acknowledgements

We would like to thank the hundreds of women we have worked with on our courses over the past twenty years, in particular the women who completed questionnaires for our survey. Not only have they helped us shape the book with their own experiences and insights, but many of their written and spoken contributions have been directly included.

We would also like to mention the busy and energetic women who have taken time to respond to our book in its rough and ready stage. Thankyou to Anna Ford, Jo Gardiner and Julia Drum.

Anita Roddick has always been a great support and a fierce champion for women's rights to self-esteem and self-confidence. We would particularly like to thank her for taking an interest in and financially supporting University research into children's self-esteem as we, like her, believe that self-confidence building work should be tackled with children at a very early age. Her foundation manager, Clive James, has also been a great source of inspiration and support for The Cause!

We would like to thank Helen Sonnet, one of our brilliant administrative team, for the background research and creative ideas she has contributed, and also Kay Hardwick for her unerring patience and inspired graphic design. We would also like to thank our families and friends for their constant help and interest in our busy lives.

The domestic work women do is often considered unimportant as it doesn't register on the standard economic indicators. Yet the new trend is to lambast mothers who go out to work. So, you're damned if you do, and damned if you don't. Or are you? Is this just a male conspiracy against working mums?

It's time to expose the myths, celebrate the working mother, and build her self-esteem. I've always said that being heard is one of the most important things for women. Not only have Eileen Gillibrand and Jenny Mosley – working mums themselves – given a voice to real working mothers in their new book, they have also given thousands of others the tools to build their own self-confidence to raise their voices even louder on the issues.

Let's banish the guilt. The new mantra to be heard is celebrate yourself as a working mother and others will do so too. The potential ripple effects of this book are irresistible ... because, like a woman's work, positive self-esteem will reach further than ever imagined, let alone acknowledged!

Anita Roddick, **founder and chief executive,** *The Body Shop*

Who is this book for?

We have written this self-help book for any working mother attempting to balance career and family life, who is keen to give time and commitment to her personal and professional development. It is our hope that the self-knowledge and insight gained by working through the practical programme will enable working mothers to boost their energy and gain equilibrium and fulfilment in their lives.

What this book offers

This self-development book has three main sections:

♦ **You – the working mother**
   This section helps you to understand yourself more completely. It enables you to take a compassionate view of yourself and to recognise the pressures and demands that may currently affect you as you strive to strike the right balance between home and work. Simple but powerful strategies for boosting your energy, thinking positively, combating negative patterns and working out successful action plans are offered.

♦ **You and your child**
   This section helps you to explore your relationship with your child and to recognise its capacity to affect all the other parts of your life. Ways of encouraging your child to become more communicative, cooperative and independent are explored.

♦ **You and your work**
   This section helps you to look at your career development. It helps you to take stock of your current situation by collecting knowledge about yourself and exploring your realistic options. It enables you to consider ways to realise your full potential (in your own eyes) through your current job or by changing direction.

How to use this book

This workbook is concerned with what you can do to help yourself. It is a self-help programme that you can work through in your own way and at your own pace, in depth over several months or over a short period of time. We would suggest that you do the exercises and complete the questionnaires as you work your way through the book and, where relevant, write down your answers. The action of writing your thoughts down on paper gives them form and structure, and records them for future reference. If you have a friend or colleague with whom to discuss the exercises, guidelines and suggestions, so much the better. Because this book has been written quite generally, for mothers working in a variety of occupations with children from toddlers to teenagers, you may sometimes need to apply the text to your own unique situation, and adapt the questionnaires and exercises to fit in with your specific needs, your child or children's age and stage, your work and the culture in which you are living.

We have tried to avoid the awkward she/he/him/her and himself/herself by alternating between our use of male and female gender.

Introduction

Why is it important to boost your energy?

Many working mothers say they lack the energy needed to make the most of their busy lives. They rush around completing an endless round of 'jobs that must be done today' at home and at work and feel cheated when they are too tired to do anything else. Consequently what they value in life, whether this is reading, going swimming with the children, having fun with their partner, learning to paint or play a musical instrument, is not being fulfilled. When our values are not being met, we can become dissatisfied, frustrated, feel guilty or depressed. Any spare energy we may have distorts into tension or flows away altogether. Guilt is a particularly destructive force in the lives of many women who choose both to work and to bring up children. When we feel guilty we start to see ourselves as victims and begin to feel powerless to change; guilt is a real energy-sapper.

Take a look at yourself, your relationships with others and your relationship with your work to assess your own energy needs.

Energy for you, your relationships and your work

* To achieve fulfilment as an individual you need energy to do those things that are personally important to you. For some women this may be to look good, with a toned body or well-chosen clothes, groomed hair and clear skin. For other women, having more energy would mean they were able to pursue chosen leisure activities, gardening, keep fit, badminton yoga, learn to paint, dance, swim or scuba dive. For some women more energy would mean being able to cope with illness, with stress at work or to manage feelings of anger and resentment. Having more energy would enable you to feel more confident to strive for an ideal and to aspire to realise your own potential.

* To achieve fulfilment in your relationships with children, family and friends takes an unending supply of energy. Some women want more energy to develop better relationships with their children, to have time for genuine communication and to give more quality attention. Organising children's parties, dealing with crying babies, coping with Christmas, children's illness, meetings with carers and teachers, helping with homework, are mentioned as times when women feel most in need of an energy boost. Relationships with partners, parents and friends are often the first things we neglect in our busy schedules. For many women a loving

relationship with their partner is fundamental to their happiness but to develop a fulfilling emotional and physical relationship with another person takes lots of energy. Some women are caring for older relatives, troubled children, dealing with issues of redundancy, infertility, poverty or homelessness. These women need a boost of energy to cope with life as it is.

✱ To achieve fulfilment in your career you need the energy to achieve a good balance between home and work. Some women have demanding jobs and are coping with busy schedules and difficult colleagues. They need energy to keep going, to be assertive and to deal with new challenges. Some women need energy to deal with the demands of career moves, with part-time schedules and unappreciative bosses; others with long hours, harassment from work colleagues and unrealistic deadlines. The needs of children, partners and parents at the end of a long day may demand the most energy of all.

How can we boost our energy?

If we want to lead a happy and fulfilling life at home and at work we must ensure that our own energy is constantly replenished. Boosting our energy is the key to gaining personal power. If we have energy we have the impetus to make things happen, the strength and motivation to strive for 'what might be'.

We can boost our energy by paying careful attention to all the different parts of our lives.

♦ We need to give time to the development of our emotional self. If we learn to build loving relationships, allow ourselves to have fun and relax with other people, then we will gain energy from the warmth of the support we give and receive.

♦ We can boost energy by taking regular physical exercise, making sure that our diet is healthy and our lifestyle balanced. Energy levels rise when we take care of our bodies through yoga, massage and relaxation.

♦ Making sure that we give time to develop our creative talents, be they music, dance or art, will release energy for us.

♦ The energy we gain from giving time to the development of our spiritual self by meditating, contemplating or practising our religious beliefs is immeasurable.

♦ Our energy levels can be replenished by giving time to the development of our cognitive self, through reading, debating, organising, planning.

Self-development is the key to a happier life

It is vital that we take positive steps to develop a calm perspective and inner strength founded on our own engagement with the process of self-development. Being told how we can help ourselves only calms our fears temporarily; voluntarily embarking on an experiential programme of self-help leads to real knowledge that can act as a touchstone of common sense when life gets tough, whether you are a working mother or not.

All human beings need to strive hard to experience the huge reservoir of joy that runs underneath life's ambushes; working mothers have to work even harder at this process. This book will support you strongly in this journey of personal and professional fulfilment.

Being unpredictable working mothers ourselves, what made us think we could write this book?

As mothers who have screamed vindictively at our children, dissolved into sobbing heaps consoled by alcohol and sympathetic friends, arrived at work with the wrong folders, whilst failing to arrive at all at the school's Harvest Festival, it seemed an enormously arrogant gesture to even think about writing a book for working mothers when many of you, we know, are doing a far better job combining their many roles than we are.

But after long conversations we realised we were falling into exactly the same downward spiral that we encourage the women we work with to avoid; we were comparing ourselves unfavourably to others, failing to give ourselves credit for the skills that we already have – to the extent that we were about to disempower ourselves completely by saying we weren't 'good enough' to write the book we knew was needed.

Because there are two of us (which supports our long held view that women's friendship is crucial) we were able logically to combat each other's fears and anxieties. We were also able to hold up each other's achievements and remind ourselves that we have spent twenty years working with women in many different ways to help them with their personal and professional development. In reality we really did have some hard-earned, oft-practised ideas and strategies learned from other women that could help women get the most out of their exciting choice of combining work with motherhood.

The women whose experiences have helped us write the book

How did we find our working mothers?

We networked through professional organisations, training courses, support groups, playgroups and schools; we talked to women who had been on our courses, work colleagues, friends, friends of friends, neighbours and students. In fact, we recruited any working mother who showed the slightest interest in the survey! We posted or gave our questionnaire to a wide range of working mothers. We asked general questions about the woman, her family and her job, how she felt about her role as a working mother, what she felt were the positive and negative effects of her working for herself and her family, and more specific questions on dealing with children and childcare, her work and career aspirations.

We found that many of the stories recounted were tantalisingly brief, and we wanted to contact further a sample of the working mothers who had responded to the questionnaire to gain more detailed information. We found a number of respondents who were willing to discuss their life as working mothers in greater detail. We visited some mothers at home individually, met others in small groups. Our sample of working mothers included women of all ages, from those with babies as young as three weeks to women whose older children had left home. We heard from women in a wide variety of jobs from school caretakers, doctors and teachers, beauticians and office workers to solicitors, computer programmers, nurses, secretaries and garden designers.

We have deliberately focused on the working mother who has at least one child in her family past the baby stage, and who is employed outside the home, because such women formed by far the largest group in our sample. When it came to deciding whom to quote and whom to leave out, we made our selection with a view to achieving as great a variety in backgrounds as possible. We asked the working mothers to say whether they minded if their names were used. We have used the first name of the women who gave us permission, and for the questionnaire returned anonymously or for women not wanting names to be used, we have used pseudonyms. Sometimes the quotation which is used to illustrate a general point is left unattributed. We owe all these working mothers a tremendous debt of gratitude for being so open in sharing their life and concerns with us.

We are both working mothers and have, through our work, always been open to listening to other working mothers about their everyday lives, at home and at work, and the pressures and pleasures of being a working mother. We have tried to give a voice in this book to these women's feelings and concerns. Women can tend to lose contact with other women as they battle through each day and imagine that they are alone coping with their insecurities, believing that others have assuaged their guilt, organised their lives, have children who are always pleasant and well-mannered, with careers that go from strength to strength. Our survey demonstrated that many of the working mothers felt they held images of other working mothers coping more easily than them! Yet in spite of tiredness, feeling overworked, difficulties with children, problems of balancing home and work, it was the overwhelming feelings of optimism, confidence and enjoyment of their busy lives which shone through.

You

This section is concerned with helping you to understand the many pressures you are under and to take positive steps towards enjoying a better quality of life.

Most of us rush around every day successfully completing a million tasks relating to our roles as mother and worker; we never really appreciate how draining and demanding our lives are. We are driven relentlessly by many forces that push us to extreme efforts without us ever realising the personal cost. Few of us fully enjoy a balanced lifestyle in which we give ourselves time to develop all aspects of our thinking, emotional, creative, physical and spiritual selves. Research has shown that even if we pursue leisure time we often fail to turn off the negative voices in our heads and therefore get no real pleasure from our 'times out'. Consequently, our energy is often low. This chapter explores all the factors holding us back from becoming a whole person and offers tried and tested ways forward.

These are just a few of the jobs that women tackle every day

How many roles do you have and try to fulfil?

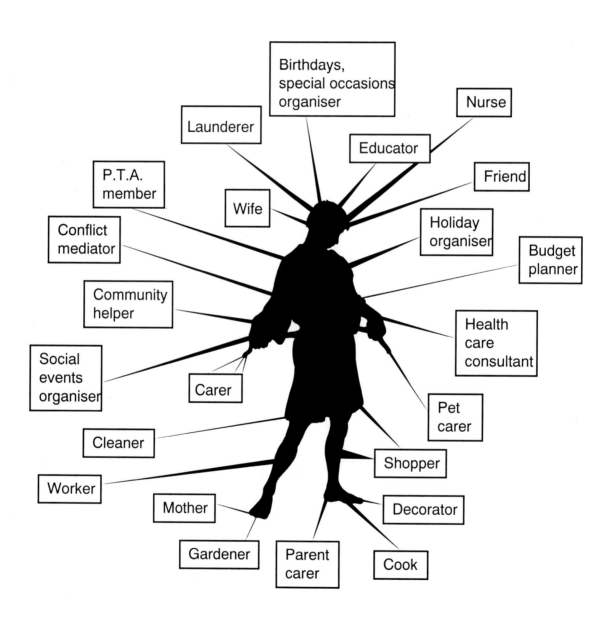

Be aware of the pressure you are under

The previous diagram illustrates the many roles that women are often expected to fulfil, a daunting prospect!. Look through the following list of commitments and tick how many you are expected to undertake; (tick if *you* normally do these things).

Organising children in the morning/evening	☐	Organising children's visits to doctors	☐
Preparing breakfasts	☐	Booking and taking children to healthcare appointments	☐
Filling the lunchboxes	☐	Attending parents' evenings at school	☐
Transporting children to and from carer/school	☐	Attending school events	☐
Grocery shopping	☐	Attending after-school social events	☐
Clothes, other items shopping	☐	Helping to organise after-school events	☐
Cleaning	☐	Any other voluntary work for school	☐
Laundry	☐	Voluntary work in the community	☐
Buying cards and presents for special occasions	☐	Visiting parents	☐
Organising social outings	☐	Shopping for parents	☐
Organising dinner parties, social events at home	☐	Cleaning for parents	☐
Booking holidays	☐	Cooking for parents	☐
Packing for holidays	☐	Caring for parents	☐
Making special purchases for holidays	☐	Preparing and cooking food	☐
Household budgeting	☐	Washing up	☐
Paying bills	☐	Meeting deadlines at work	☐
Organising finances for other family members	☐	Having to work overtime/weekends	☐

Decorating in the home	☐	Organising work clothes	☐
Organising repair work for home/domestic appliances	☐	Organising other people at work	☐
Helping children with homework	☐	Meeting senior manager's demands	☐
Nursing sick children	☐	Promoting client/customer relationships	☐
Conflict mediator between children	☐	Initiating new projects at work	☐
Conflict mediator between husband and children	☐	Dealing with enquiries at work	☐
Visiting friends	☐	Reading journals, joining associations to keep up with latest developments at work	☐
Entertaining friends at home	☐	Maintaining equipment at work	☐
Caring for pets	☐	Entertaining business colleagues	☐
Organising veterinary visits	☐	Updating technological skills	☐
Gardening	☐	Completing projects/items of work at home	☐
Bathing, washing children	☐	Making work-related telephone calls from home	☐
Travelling to and from work	☐	Attending out-of-hours work courses/conferences etc.	☐
Organising work-related social events	☐	Purchasing items for work outside hours	☐

Were you shocked by the number of roles you perform?

Now you have taken a realistic look at the many and varied demands that working mothers may be subjected to, it is hardly surprising that you often feel under enormous pressure. This book intends to focus on the personal demands and conflicts that occur when women try to be good mothers and also have to fulfil important responsibilities at work. It considers ways forward to help you feel calmer and more content with your life.

Firstly we will consider the ideas that drive you in both these roles, and start by looking at where these ideals originate from. One influencing factor is the views of other important people in our lives, especially if we respect and admire them. The following section illustrates the sorts of thing we might hear from other people regarding motherhood and work and how this can affect us.

What women told us

'I feel like a hamster on a wheel – forever moving but getting nowhere.'

'An ideal mother is someone who can juggle housework, work, bringing up children and remain SANE.'

'I just never catch up on all the jobs that need to be done.'

Jane's story

Sometimes it's like we're all in a pressure cooker. I feel that any minute the lid is going to blow off and my life will explode in all directions. Everyone seems to expect me to fulfil all my duties like some sort of automaton; I can't have an off-day or forget to do something without incurring someone's displeasure. I don't think any of them realise just how much I actually get done each day or how many different 'hats' I have to wear to deal with all the different situations in my life.

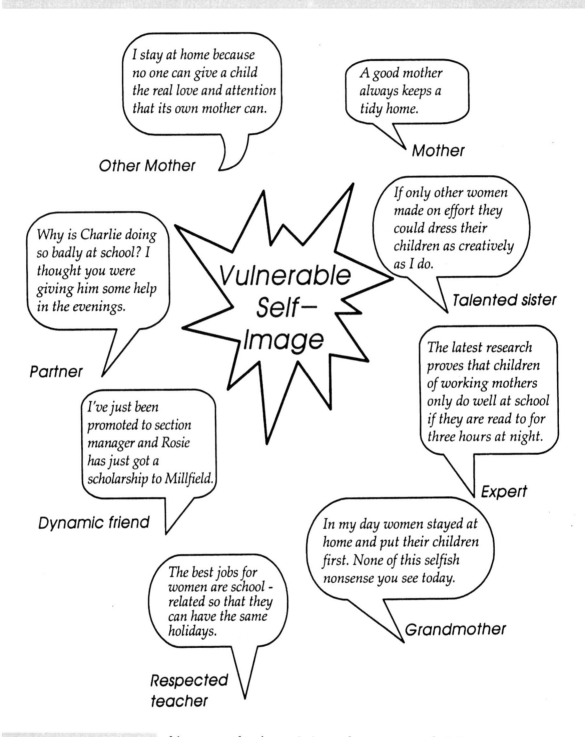

Other Mother: *I stay at home because no one can give a child the real love and attention that its own mother can.*

Mother: *A good mother always keeps a tidy home.*

Talented sister: *If only other women made on effort they could dress their children as creatively as I do.*

Partner: *Why is Charlie doing so badly at school? I thought you were giving him some help in the evenings.*

Vulnerable Self–Image

Expert: *The latest research proves that children of working mothers only do well at school if they are read to for three hours at night.*

Dynamic friend: *I've just been promoted to section manager and Rosie has just got a scholarship to Millfield.*

Grandmother: *In my day women stayed at home and put their children first. None of this selfish nonsense you see today.*

Respected teacher: *The best jobs for women are school - related so that they can have the same holidays.*

Your mother's voice Your mother's opinions have seeped into your very soul often without you even realising this. Consequently there are times when you make choices e.g. to leave the house in a mess in order to go out for a picnic, but instead of enjoying the spontaneity of the occasion you are accompanied by a continual sense of guilt, because your mother would disapprove of this decision. It's difficult to become your own person, if your mother continues to treat you to her opinions.

Other mothers' voices We are often impressed with the group of mothers who meet at the school gates, manage to attend every school function, make stupendous fancy dress costumes, and always appear holding hands with or pushing other immaculately dressed children. Their comments about motherhood can often cut you to the quick as they are proud of their decision to stay at home and are often loudly condemning of mothers who have chosen to work.

Talented sister's voice It's amazing how influenced we are by the talents and qualities of our brothers and sisters; often comparing ourselves unfavourably to them. Because you come from the same family stock there is a sneaking feeling that, possessing the same genes and parentage, you also ought to be capable of the same achievements.

Partner's voice It takes a very balanced, wise man to fully understand the difficulties experienced by a working mother. Many men appear liberated and sometimes very helpful, nevertheless they often, like their mothers, harbour ingrained ideals of how women should be with their children. We're often unprepared for the devastating pang of guilt that shoots through us when our partner is disappointed or disparaging about the quality of our parenting. So hurt are we that we often don't see the unfairness of the remark.

Experts' voices With the growth of technology and the media, we are now – unlike our predecessors – surrounded by research and reports about the devastating effect we as working mothers can have upon our children. No sooner are we convinced that we have already seriously damaged our child's future potential, than we have another opinion forced down our throats. We are bombarded with 'The best mothers do it this way' books or 'How to make your child successful' books. All in all the media presents us with a minefield of information, whatever we do or don't do is condemned by somebody.

Respected teacher's voice Often the dynamic role-models presented to us by the teachers that we have come into contact with in the past have a huge impact on us. Being young and vulnerable we tend to take their ideas seriously, hence many of us were guided in a very limited way towards women's 'type' occupations, e.g. teaching, nursing, secretarial. But even their stray and random comments were given huge prestige especially if we respected and admired them.

Grandmother's voice Some 'elders' in the family have a long speech within them about how life used to be. There is something very seductive about the world they paint. You can 'smell' the freshly baked bread, picture the roses round the door, hear the murmur of children's voices as they tell each other stories, feel the warmth and glow of the log fire and taste the dumplings in the nourishing stew. Life was simple, supportive and straightforward! This powerful image of past motherhood – rosy-cheeked, beaming smile and floury hands – is still beckoning us today. It's an exceptionally hard ideal to combat as our very soul seems to yearn for the pace and simplicity it offers, whilst we conveniently forget how life has drastically changed through industrialisation and technology

Dynamic friend's voice These friends have often been with us since childhood. Attractive, confident and extremely capable, they seem not to burst into tears or grab the bottle of wine in the early evening or row with their children. Their achievements are hard to reject as they themselves, in addition to being competent, are often thoughtful, sensitive and supportive to us. We can't even dismiss them as being hard-nosed 'bitches', as we know they are caring and affectionate. Their encouragement and understanding of us can be utterly depressing when underneath we feel a complete wreck.

Voices that haunt us – at work

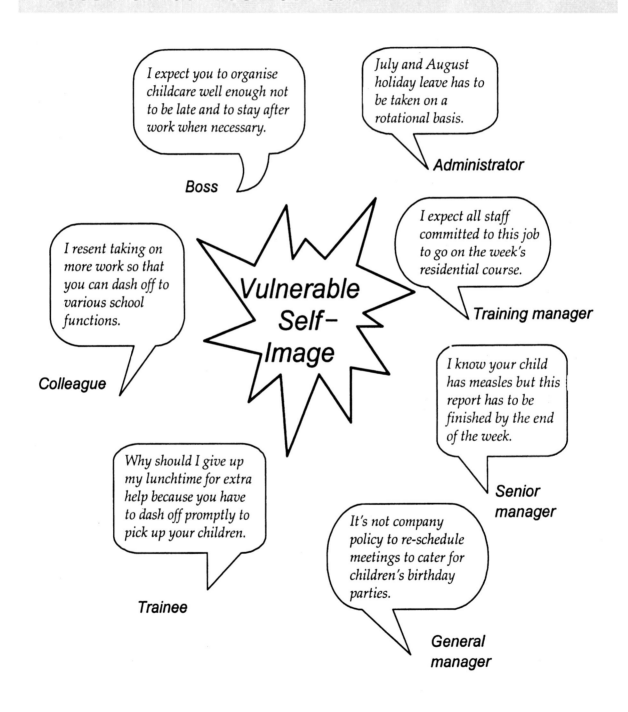

I expect you to organise childcare well enough not to be late and to stay after work when necessary.
Boss

July and August holiday leave has to be taken on a rotational basis.
Administrator

I resent taking on more work so that you can dash off to various school functions.
Colleague

Vulnerable Self-Image

I expect all staff committed to this job to go on the week's residential course.
Training manager

I know your child has measles but this report has to be finished by the end of the week.
Senior manager

Why should I give up my lunchtime for extra help because you have to dash off promptly to pick up your children.
Trainee

It's not company policy to re-schedule meetings to cater for children's birthday parties.
General manager

Administrator's voice For many administrators, arranging staff holidays is an eternal headache, with employees all competing for the same weeks. If this kind of system operates in your workplace, you will be expected to take your place in the queue for choosing time off, regardless of the fact that you have children. This can cause dilemmas if your time off does not coincide with school holidays, i.e. should you remove your children from school during term time to take a family holiday?

Training manager's voice From the training manager's point of view, if you have elected to work in this company you should be willing and available to attend any necessary training courses. She will not want to hear that you cannot attend because your child has chicken pox, is going through a 'clingy' phase or your childminder has suddenly let you down. This area can be fraught with problems and stress, as you try to juggle all the necessary arrangements that will enable you to have the time required of you.

Colleague's voice Colleagues can be very sympathetic to the problems you encounter as a working mother, until the problems affect them. If their workload or stress level is increased because you are unable to fulfil responsibilities for a child-related reason, their goodwill may quickly evaporate. Colleagues who feel you are not pulling your weight may soon become resentful and question whether, considering your maternal duties, you should be employed in the first place. Working mothers often feel enormous guilt if they know they are letting colleagues down when they have to take time off for their children.

Trainee's voice Trainees, too, can feel very put out if their programmes are affected or interrupted by your maternal duties. Often younger and childless, they have little patience or understanding over the problems that can arise from being a working mother. You may feel guilty that you are not giving them the time and commitment they deserve.

Boss's voice Your immediate boss will have pressures from both above and below – i.e. from both senior managers and your colleagues. Middle management can be very precarious and stressful and people in this position do not want their burdens added to through workers having child-related problems. Your relationship with your boss will influence much of what happens at work, e.g. your enjoyment of work, your chances of promotion, the goodwill your boss extends to you. Many women are terrified of souring this relationship and experience considerable stress when there is a conflict of loyalties between their children and their boss. Whichever choice they make can leave them feeling guilty.

Senior manager's voice Senior managers will be looking for successful results from their sections or departments. Even if the senior manager knows you, this knowledge will probably be fairly superficial and based on facts and figures, rather than personalities. As you become less of a real person in the hierarchy, your personal problems and dilemmas will receive less consideration and sympathy. To the senior manager you may just be a cog in a wheel of the machine. All that matters is your ability to keep that wheel moving and not slow down or stop the motion.

General manager's voice The general manager's concern is with the corporate image of his company. There may be many instructions and exhortations from this exalted position, but often very little concern for individuals. The general manager usually just takes an overview of how the company is doing: any 'fly in the ointment' is dealt with in the company's best interest.

Which 'voices' influence your Ideals?

All the 'voices' that you hear talking about ideals of both motherhood and your work role influence and affect how you perceive them. We will now look at the various voices that have had an impact on you. *Fill in the people and the views that you consider have most shaped the ideals you hold for being a good mother.*

Now complete a similar diagram writing in the people and the views that have most influenced your work ideals.

In addition to these important voices there are probably many other ideals that you are driven by, perhaps without even realising how greatly they actually do influence you.

Look through the two sets on the following pages and tick all the ideals that you strive for.

Keep the house clean and tidy............ ☐

Prepare well-balanced meals............... ☐

Pay attention to my children's
appearance.................................... ☐

Be calm at all times......................... ☐

Have time to listen to my
children... ☐

Know when my children are
worried... ☐

Be committed to helping with my
children's education.......................... ☐

Allow my children their point of
view... ☐

Appreciate how big my
children's problems are to them........... ☐

Understand my children's peer
culture.. ☐

Exercise discipline fairly..................... ☐

Not allow anger to cloud my
judgement...................................... ☐

Say sorry when I am in the wrong....... ☐

Not use emotional blackmail
against my children........................... ☐

Be patient when my children are
slow... ☐

Be understanding when my
children are tired and crotchety........... ☐

Be supportive and caring when
my children are unwell....................... ☐

Spend time with my children in
shared activities................................... ☐

Show my children a calm
smiling face....................................... ☐

Teach behaviour by showing a
good example...................................... ☐

Overcome my tiredness to be fair
to my children.................................... ☐

Not let my children see when I
am worried.. ☐

Be aware of all that is happening
in my children's lives........................... ☐

Always attend school functions.......... ☐

Invite my children's friends to
my house... ☐

Organise leisure activities for my
children... ☐

Put my children's needs before
my own... ☐

Always know what to say to my
children... ☐

Consider my appearance so that
my children are not embarrassed
by it... ☐

Become involved in school-
parent's associations .... ☐

Help with school functions................. ☐

In my work role I feel that it is important that I should ...

Be punctual...☐

Never shirk any duties ....☐

Give 100% effort to my duties ....☐

Be on time in meeting deadlines ....☐

Show respect towards and
interest in all colleagues ....☐

Be fair and consistent with
colleagues ....☐

Maintain an interest in my job..............☐

Be willing to offer additional
help/time in emergencies ....☐

Be creative in new initiatives................☐

Deal efficiently and patiently
with clients/customers..........................☐

Be positive in my attitude to
work..☐

Not allow home problems to
distract me at work................................☐

Live up to my boss's expectations.......☐

Give consideration to my
appearance...☐

Be willing to offer time/energy to
social functions.......................................☐

Be sensitive to colleague's
problems ....☐

Be loyal to my boss/company.............☐

Not burden colleagues with my
problems ....☐

Appear cheerful and contented...........☐

What women told us

Jane: *'I feel guilty if I cannot be with my children when they really need me.'*
Angela: *'I always feel annoyed at the mess in my home.'*
Joanna: *'I feel very bad when people make comments about me not being a 'real' mother because I work.'*

Angie's story

I wish I could be less sensitive to how other people see me and the comments they sometimes make. I know I can't be perfect, but I feel I don't quite fit in to either role properly because of the demands of the other role. I feel pulled between wanting to be seen just as a mother, when I'm in my home role and wanting to be just a worker when I'm with my colleagues. If I forget something I'd like people to just accept that I'm sometimes forgetful and not blame it on either the fact that I work or that I have children.

The ideal self versus the actual self

Our ideal selves, both at work and as mothers, are often a far cry from reality as the following cameos illustrate.

Ideal self

Your cricket whites are washed, ironed and hanging in your wardrobe, darling.

→

Actual self

Your cricket whites are on the bathroom floor where you left them last week.

Ideal self

Here's your tea, children – free-range eggs, low-fat mayonnaise, cress, wholemeal bread, home-made flapjacks, thickly-sliced carrots, celery and cucumber (all organically grown), and fresh fruit that I picked from dear old Mr Cobbley's orchard.

→

Actual self

Here's your tea, children – pie and chips I picked up on the way home and a bottle of Coke.

Actual self

The hamster was actually decomposing. Rover ran off again and Tabby had kittens in the airing cupboard.

Ideal self

We won top prize for the healthiest-looking hamster, Rover's just completed dog obedience classes and we've taught Tabby to play hide and seek.

→

Actual self

Molly arrived late at the boardroom, desperately trying to shuffle the papers of her report into some sort of coherent order. Suddenly she became aware of the grubby child's fingermarks on her blouse.

Ideal self

Molly entered the boardroom briskly, confident her report was brilliant and her appearance a 'knockout'.

→

Ideal self	Actual self
Amy glanced at the school notice appealing for help from mothers with the forthcoming fete and immediately signed her name.	Amy groaned inwardly at the sight of another school appeal for volunteer mothers, thinking she must be the only mother who was never available to help.
Carol discussed the latest fashions and the merits of current bands with her teenage daughter, feeling that she was really up-together with the trends.	'Turn down that racket and you can't possibly go out looking like that!' shrieked Carol to her teenage daughter, who yelled back, 'Get a life, Mum, I can't wait to leave home'.
Despite a horrendous day at work, Anna smiled at her young son and sat with him on the sofa so that he could relate his day to her.	'Leave me alone now, I'll talk to you in a minute,' muttered Anna, wishing she could drown her horrendous day at work in alcohol and oblivion.
Poppy's fancy dress outfit is stunning, thought Cassie, 'Even if it did take me a fortnight to make.'	'Please God let the safety pins in Poppy's outfit hold it together,' thought Cassie.

Ideal self

'Don't worry, John, I'll deal with Mrs Jackson,' offered Kate, 'I know what an old dragon she is.'

Actual self

'John, I can't face Mrs Jackson after a night up with Sam. You'll have to deal with her,' moaned Kate.

Ideal self

'Yes Jake, of course I'll help you with your maths homework.'

Actual self

'Jake, I've been at work all day, I'm too tired to help you with your maths. Ask your father, brother, uncle, grandpa anyone else to give you a hand.'

Ideal self

Emma thought happily that she was making a real success of this evening's do; she knew both her boss and the senior manager had found her conversation witty and entertaining.

Actual self

Emma lurked in the corner of McDonald's hoping that she wouldn't be seen by anyone from work. She had claimed 'flu' to excuse her from the work's do, so that she could celebrate her son's birthday with him.

Ideal self

Today was a holiday! Sarah and the children were going to enjoy a leisurely picnic in idyllic surroundings. They would feel carefree and ecstatically happy.

Actual self

Today was a holiday! Sarah was going to clean the pigsty of a home, while the children moaned how bored they were. They would all feel miserable and thoroughly bad-tempered.

Recap

We all have ideal selves: those gleaming images of smiles, endless patience, boundless energy, total empathy and absolute wisdom. We also often fall very short of these ideal selves because we are human and the world in which we live is not ideal. Generally, we accept that this is reality and therefore only to be expected, but at certain times or in certain areas of our lives, the mismatch between our ideal and actual selves is too great for us to be comfortable with. The gaping chasm we perceive can make us feel hopeless and guilty.

Guilt, frustration and resentment are probably the most common feelings that working mothers experience. You are especially likely to have these feelings if you hold negative views or beliefs about any aspects of your roles. Look through the following list of statements and tick any that reflect your own views or beliefs.

What negative views do you hold about your roles?

I don't want to work, but we need the money .... ☐

Having children has interfered with my career prospects .... ☐

My mother thinks I'm dreadful for leaving the children with a childminder .... ☐

My partner says I'm lazy if I don't work .... ☐

No one ever helps me with the housework .... ☐

I'm not a maternal person .... ☐

Non-working mothers think my children suffer because I work .... ☐

Being at home with the children bores me .... ☐

My children don't like me going to work .... ☐

Work makes me too tired to be a good mother .... ☐

I can never satisfy both my family's and work needs .... ☐

I think my working will have an adverse effect on my children .... ☐

My children don't appreciate the benefits of my working .... ☐

My children compare me unfavourably with mothers who don't work .... ☐

My children complain when I bring work home .... ☐

Because I work, I've missed lots of 'milestones' in my children's lives ...... ☐

No minder could love and care for my children as well as I could .... ☐

I feel really bad about working in school holidays .... ☐

No-one understands how tired I get .... ☐

My family don't give me any credit for my success at work .... ☐

No one appreciates all the effort I make .... ☐

People at work don't understand the problems of being a working mother .... ☐

My family don't support me when I'm having a bad time .... ☐

I feel I'm selfish because I want a career .... ☐

I have problems with my children's behaviour because I'm working.......... ☐

My children expect me to buy them anything they want because I work.... ☐

I feel left out of school functions .... ☐

I feel envious of colleagues who don't have children .... ☐

I feel bad about missing work if the children are ill .... ☐

I neglect my children's healthcare appointments because of work............ ☐

I won't be promoted because I have young children .... ☐

Were you surprised by how many ticks you put down?

Your views will reflect the way you behave and, unfortunately, negative feelings often lead to negative responses, which fail to deal effectively with the current situation and may encourage an escalation of your negative feelings and behaviour. The following three examples show this in practice.

Negative feelings leading to negative behaviour

Example 1

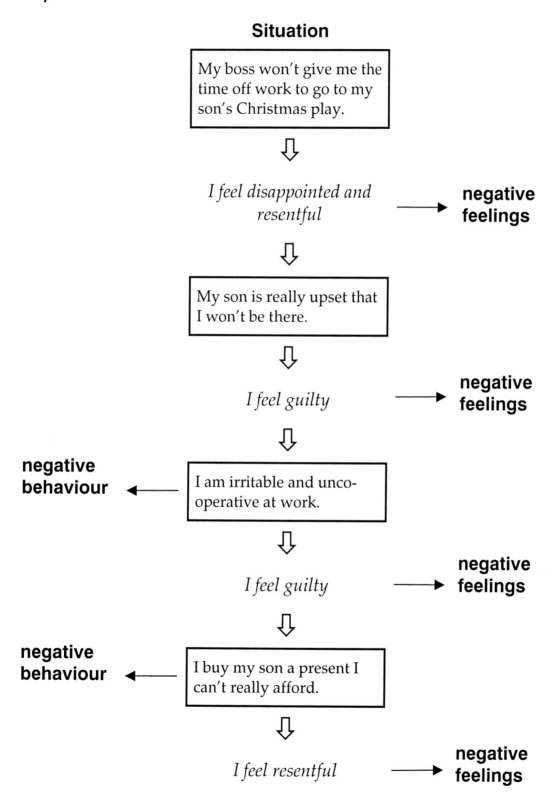

Situation

My boss won't give me the time off work to go to my son's Christmas play.

⬇

I feel disappointed and resentful ⟶ **negative feelings**

⬇

My son is really upset that I won't be there.

⬇

I feel guilty ⟶ **negative feelings**

⬇

negative behaviour ⟵ I am irritable and unco-operative at work.

⬇

I feel guilty ⟶ **negative feelings**

⬇

negative behaviour ⟵ I buy my son a present I can't really afford.

⬇

I feel resentful ⟶ **negative feelings**

Example 2

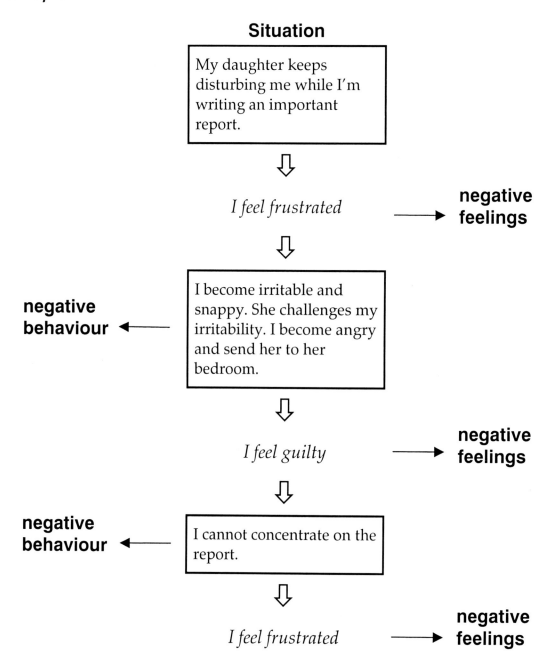

Situation

My daughter keeps
disturbing me while I'm
writing an important
report.

⇩

I feel frustrated ⟶ **negative feelings**

⇩

I become irritable and
snappy. She challenges my
irritability. I become angry
and send her to her
bedroom.

negative behaviour ⟵

⇩

I feel guilty ⟶ **negative feelings**

⇩

I cannot concentrate on the
report.

negative behaviour ⟵

⇩

I feel frustrated ⟶ **negative feelings**

Example 3

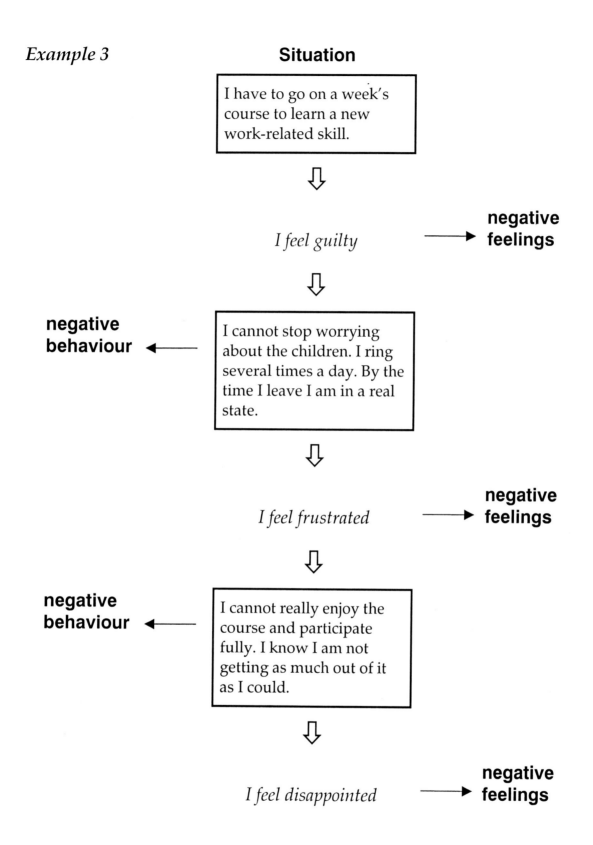

Situation

I have to go on a week's course to learn a new work-related skill.

⇩

I feel guilty ⟶ **negative feelings**

⇩

negative behaviour ⟵ I cannot stop worrying about the children. I ring several times a day. By the time I leave I am in a real state.

⇩

I feel frustrated ⟶ **negative feelings**

⇩

negative behaviour ⟵ I cannot really enjoy the course and participate fully. I know I am not getting as much out of it as I could.

⇩

I feel disappointed ⟶ **negative feelings**

Now look at these same three examples re-written to show how a positive response to a negative feeling can deal effectively with a situation and lead to a positive feeling.

Example 1

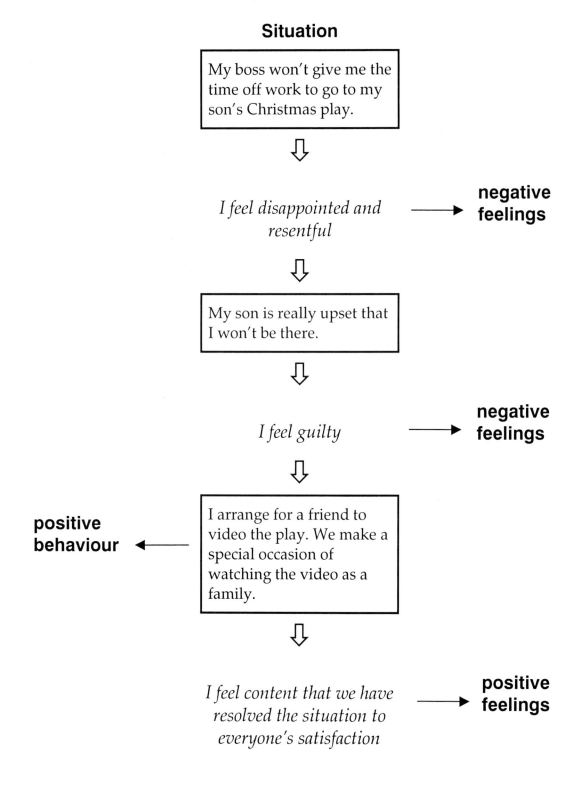

Situation

My boss won't give me the
time off work to go to my
son's Christmas play.

⬇

*I feel disappointed and
resentful*   ⟶   **negative
feelings**

⬇

My son is really upset that
I won't be there.

⬇

I feel guilty   ⟶   **negative
feelings**

⬇

**positive
behaviour** ⟵ I arrange for a friend to
video the play. We make a
special occasion of
watching the video as a
family.

⬇

*I feel content that we have
resolved the situation to
everyone's satisfaction*   ⟶   **positive
feelings**

Example 2

Situation

My daughter keeps
disturbing me while I'm
writing an important
report.

⇩

I feel frustrated ⟶ **negative
feelings**

⇩

I explain that I would
rather spend the time with
her, but the report must be
completed today. We
discuss what she would
like to do while I am busy.
She decides to write a
'report' on her school. We
work quietly together.

**positive
behaviour** ⟵

⇩

*I feel relieved that I can
get on with the report
and pleased that my
daughter is happily
occupied* ⟶ **positive
feelings**

Example 3   **Situation**

```
┌─────────────────────────┐
│ I have to go on a week's │
│ course to learn a new    │
│ work-related skill.      │
└─────────────────────────┘
```

⇩

I feel guilty ⟶ **negative feelings**

⇩

```
┌─────────────────────────┐
│ I talk through my week's │
│ absence with the children.│
│ They understand why I    │
│ have to go and are happy │
│ with the arrangements I  │
│ have made for them. I will│
│ ring every evening to talk│
│ to them.                 │
└─────────────────────────┘
```

positive behaviour ⟵

⇩

I feel happy that the children will be well cared for and accept my absence ⟶ **positive feelings**

⇩

```
┌─────────────────────────┐
│ I am able to enjoy the   │
│ course and fully         │
│ participate.             │
└─────────────────────────┘
```

positive behaviour ⟵

⇩

I feel pleased and satisfied that I have gained maximum potential from the course ⟶ **positive feelings**

Recap

You cannot eliminate negative feelings from your life, but by responding to them in a positive way you can deal effectively with a situation and avoid a negative spiral developing, which would make the situation worse. By learning to make a positive response you will, moreover, be able to dispel the negative feeling and replace it with a positive one.

Exploring guilt further

It would be unrealistic to expect that, as working mothers, we would never feel pangs of guilt that our children are somehow 'missing out' because we work. However, constant guilt is draining for you or your family because it will lead you to behave in negative ways. Most people react to guilt in one of the following ways:

♦ by trying to compensate

♦ by becoming defensive

♦ by trying to shift the guilt onto someone else

We will look at each of these responses more closely and see how they lead to negative situations.

Trying to compensate

If we deal with guilt by trying to make amends, this all too often means that because we are feeling bad about ourselves – i.e. for making our children suffer, we are prepared to suffer in order to redress the balance. We might, for example, be overly tolerant of our children's behaviour, saying to ourselves, 'It's only natural that they behave badly when they're with me, because I've been away from them for so long.' We are, in fact, accepting the bad behaviour as our punishment to redress the balance. We might become slaves to our children's every whim to try and atone for our work absences, or spend vast amounts of money on toys and entertainments. Some mothers devote all their non-working time to their children, leaving none for themselves, in an effort to make amends for the time they spend at work. All of these ways of making amends are unhealthy as they encourage selfishness and lack of sensitivity in our children.

Becoming defensive

A second way of dealing with guilt is by becoming defensive. Although you might be aware that you have said or done something you do not really agree with, or perhaps neglected to do something you should have done, you will defend yourself in order to remove any guilt you might otherwise feel. If you can justify your actions to yourself and others then you will have no cause to feel guilty.

Shifting the guilt

We all feel very much better if we can shift our burden of guilt onto someone else. If, for example, our children complain about our working, we might try and place any guilt we feel squarely back onto their shoulders by informing them that we only work for their benefit, to provide them with nice clothes, holidays etc. The problem with shifting guilt onto someone else is that they then have this uncomfortable burden, which they in turn have to get rid of.

How do you respond to guilt?

Think of typical scenarios that make you feel guilty. Fill in the boxes with your usual responses, then consider whether these have a positive or negative outcome.

Situations that make me feel guilty	How I respond	What outcome does my response have
Example: Forgetting to organise babysitting well ahead	I become bad tempered and snappy	I alienate everyone else with my bad temper
Example: Taking unscheduled time off work	I behave like a martyr with my partner because its me not him who has missed work	He becomes guilty and defensive

If you feel that your responses to guilt have a negative consequence, you need to find more positive ways of responding. The next section shows how this can be achieved.

Don't allow other people to make you feel guilty

Quite often our guilt arises from the comments other people make to us, which either reflect areas that we have neglected or highlight areas where we do not achieve as highly as they do. If you felt perfectly happy with a situation before someone sowed seeds of doubt and guilt, you need firstly to ask yourself if the guilt is really justified. The fact that other people have different values and priorities to you, does not necessarily make yours wrong. Have a bit more confidence in your right to make the choices in life that suit you and that you believe in, and try not to let other people foist their views and attitudes onto you.

Accept the fact that you are a working mother

There are probably many situations in your life which are not necessarily ideal, but which you accept as facts and which, therefore, do not give rise to feelings of guilt. Consider some of the following:

♦ The area in which you live

♦ The house in which you live

♦ The number of children you have

♦ Your relatives, etc

The fact is that you do work and, like many other situations in life, it is not always ideal. Forget what is ideal and learn to focus on work as just another fact of your life which you and other people need to accept.

Focus on the positive when things are bad

If you experience a really bad patch, when everything about being a working mother seems to be negative, have a prepared list ready that highlights all the positive aspects of work. (Make this list when you are feeling good, as if you are feeling negative nothing can seem worthwhile.)

The list below will give you some idea of positive aspects you might include.

♦ My family benefits financially

♦ Work provides me with an interest

♦ I enjoy the company of my colleagues

♦ I use skills at work that I would not otherwise have the opportunity to practise

♦ I increase my knowledge and skill level by going to work

♦ I enjoy financial independence by working

♦ I enjoy the status of my work role

When you are feeling low, talk yourself through the list you have made and remind yourself of all the positive benefits of working. You might even enlist the help of someone else to read your list to you and help you focus again on the positive aspects.

Learning to respond to guilt more appropriately

There will of course be occasions when you feel justifiably guilty, e.g. breaking a promise to your children, letting work colleagues down, not keeping to your usual standards of housekeeping, etc. If, by now, you realise that your response to guilt is not really appropriate or helpful you can learn to deal with guilt in a way that is more positive to both yourself and others by following the steps set out below.

You don't have to be perfect

> If you are striving for perfection at work and as a mother, forget it! As human beings, we are all fallible and no one realistically expects perfection. If you set standards that are too high to maintain, you are inviting trouble and condemnation from both yourself and others.

Acknowledge how other people feel

> If someone is hurt, angered or feels resentful because of your actions, it always helps them to know that you are aware of and understand their feelings. Instead of trying to ignore how others feel or responding with negative feelings yourself, learn to say calmly 'I know you are feeling angry because I did/did not ...'
> Even if you don't feel their reaction has been justified, a response that acknowledges how other people feel can work wonders in defusing a situation and allow you both to put aside negative feelings.

❸ *Saying 'sorry'*

So many people find it impossible to say this one little word – why? Saying 'sorry' means that you acknowledge you are in the wrong (especially difficult for perfectionists), and can often open the door to further accusations or demands from others. Saying 'sorry' is in fact the best way to admit your mistake. When the apology is genuine and you also acknowledge others' feelings, it provides the most secure basis to resolve a situation. Saying 'sorry' does not mean you have to make unrealistic recompense, only that you are aware of and feel remorse for your actions. Also, it becomes easier the more frequently you practise it.

❹ *Look for a positive response to guilt*

When you react to guilt, first consider your response and its consequences. Are you setting up a precedent for future occasions? For example, if you buy your child a new toy to make up for a disappointment, will this become an expectation. Is your response appropriate to the situation? Will your response lead to a satisfactory outcome for all parties concerned? Has your response adequately dealt with your guilt?

Learn to recognise and discard negative responses and replace them with more positive ones.

What women told us

Jenny: *'Most of the time I feel guilty about something or another that I haven't done.*
Sally: *'Rory has this way of looking really pitiful and dejected when I've let him down; I think he really plays the poor hard-done-by soul for all its worth to make me feel bad.'*
Nona: *'Guilt's a funny thing, very easy to acquire and very difficult to get rid of.'*

Dealing with resentment and anger

As with guilt, it would be unrealistic to expect you will never feel angry or resentful. However, if you harbour a continual resentment or anger, it will be easily sparked off by any trigger event. You are therefore in danger of 'flare ups' at any time, which will affect your own and others' lives.

Looking at resentment

Resentment arises when we consider a situation or other people's behaviour is unfair. From our point of view, harbouring resentment is unhealthy as it leads to prejudice and other negative behaviours. We need therefore to find ways of dealing effectively with resentment.

Is your resentment based on an unrealistic appraisal?

Sometimes people become resentful when others don't behave in a way they feel is appropriate or considerate. However, if this is a matter of personal views and priorities then perhaps it is you and not other people who is being unfair. Ask yourself honestly whether these people have any less right to their opinions than you have. Perhaps you need to learn to be more tolerant and accept that everyone is different.

Talking it through

Talking about your resentment can be helpful. It may be that other people are unaware that their actions are making you feel resentful. They may be willing to change their behaviour or find a compromise that would be acceptable to you both. At the least, discussion would clarify their motives and help you take appropriate action.

Find a balance

If someone refuses to be considerate, try and find an appropriate way that might lead to a change in their behaviour or in some way redress the balance for you. For example, if your children refuse to put dirty washing in the laundry basket, don't do it for them, let them run out of clean clothes. If your partner refuses to help with household chores, do only those that affect you or use part of your salary (which might provide privileges for your partner) to pay for a home help.

Does your behaviour invite lack of consideration?

Examine your behaviour carefully (even ask for your friends' comments) to see whether you are making it easy for other people to 'put upon' you. Are you always willing to do more than your fair share, do you let other people take advantage of you, do you take the seemingly easier option of putting up with unfairness to avoid confrontations? Perhaps you need to learn to be more assertive in your dealings with others in order to avoid situations that will lead to resentment.

Advice note: Make a list of the areas in your life that cause you to feel resentful. Determine that you will deal with them, one at a time. If it helps, write out a progress chart of the steps you take and 'stick to your guns' when you are 'helping' others to become more considerate.

Learning to express anger effectively

There is nothing wrong with feeling angry, but how we express our anger can be damaging to both ourselves and others. It is very easy, in the heat of the moment, to lash out verbally and even physically, causing hurt to others and often leaving ourselves remorseful, once we have calmed down.

If you feel that you and others suffer from your temper, you can learn to handle anger in a more effective way. First, you need to realise that other people can't make you angry. Anger is your response to other people or situations based on your personal expectations. You need to examine these expectations to see if they are fair and justified. Perhaps adjusting your own view or learning to tolerate the view of others would help dilute the anger you feel. It might be a good idea to write down the occasions that lead you to become angry and see if any patterns of behaviour emerge, You may have become locked into a cycle of confrontations with someone and are repeating negative responses set off by the same or similar triggers. If this is the case it is possible to write a new scenario, if you can both look at the problem in a spirit of mutual respect and cooperation.

Advice note: You might also find it helpful to write down all the things that make you angry and why. Sometimes, understanding the reasons can help us deal with or learn to avoid confrontational situations.

Learning to manage anger

There are many ways in which you can learn to manage your anger so that your responses can become constructive rather than destructive.

Counting slowly to ten is a very simple but effective method of giving yourself a little time to calm down before you respond.

Learn a short relaxation technique that you can practise anywhere, when you feel the tension rising.

More positive ways forward

This section deals with other considerations and ways forward to help you manage your life more effectively and cope with the many demands that are made on you.

Examine your stress levels

Too high a level of stress will undoubtedly have an adverse effect on your health and your ability to cope with life. Below are some of the negative effects that high levels of stress can produce.

Physical effects include:

- headaches
- tiredness
- exhaustion
- weight loss
- stomach upsets and ulcers
- aching muscles
- susceptibility to infections
- heart disease

Cognitive effects include:

- inability to concentrate
- impaired memory
- greater liability to make errors
- reduction in ability to assess and predict accurately
- paranoia

Emotional effects include:

- inability to relax
- increase in emotional outbursts
- increase in personality disorders
- increase in feelings of worthlessness
- increase in feelings of hopelessness

Negative coping responses increase stress

Causes of stress

Ill-health	Family pressures	Environmental pressures
Pain	Emotional pressures	Social pressures
Change	Work pressures	Decision-making
Travel	Financial pressures	Phobias

Stress can result in negative personal changes

 for example:

Physical changes	*Thinking and emotional changes*	*Behavioural changes*
Tension	Poor concentration	Irritability
Tiredness	Anxiety	Emotional outbursts
Illness	Depression	Poor eating habits
		Drug and alcohol abuse

 leads to

Ill-health	Nervous breakdown	Rushing from one thing to another
Psychosomatic illness	Insomnia	Becoming obsessional
		Drug/alcohol dependency

 which in turn leads to

Inability to cope with future pressures and stress
Breakdown in relationships
Feelings of physical disharmony
Reduced productivity
Prolonged mental illness
Physical and emotional vulnerability
Lack of fulfilment and loss of happiness

Positive coping responses reduce stress

Causes of stress

Ill-health	Family pressures	Environmental pressures
Pain	Emotional pressures	Social pressures
Change	Work pressures	Decision-making
Travel	Financial pressures	Phobias

Making the following personal responses helps you to cope in a positive way

 for example:

Physical responses	*Thinking and emotional responses*	*Behavioural responses*
Healthy eating Relaxation Exercise	Talking honestly to people Learning to think positively	Going to assertiveness course Efficient use of time Changing your circumstances

 leads to

Better physical health	Mental and emotional well-being	Greater self-confidence

 which in turn leads to

Ability to cope with future pressures and stress Healthier relationships Feelings of physical well-being Greater productivity Increased happiness and fulfilment

Five steps to combat stress

1. Be more disciplined with yourself

If you are the kind of person who is always volunteering for tasks or engaging in numerous activities you may need to take a long, hard look at whether you are biting off more than you can chew. If you are giving yourself more headaches than enjoyment you need to learn to inject a little realism into your decisions and live your life at a more comfortable pace. Evaluate the choices you make more thoroughly to see if the benefits really outweigh the hassles, and become more disciplined in rejecting those that don't. If your life became less hectic you would have more time and energy to enjoy it.

2. Learn to delegate

Learn the art of when and how to delegate jobs to others and thereby reduce the pressure on yourself. If you are generally doing too much, either at work or at home, you need to talk to the other people involved and explain this to them. Find ways that they or others can take on some of your tasks even if this means you have to lower your standards a little – e.g. the children's washing up may not be as good as yours, but if it's good enough, does it really matter as much as your well-being? Don't be a martyr when you are ill or under extreme pressure. Ask for and expect others to be helpful.

3. Relax your standards at crisis times

Instead of adding to your burdens in times of crisis, learn to relax your standards and 'let things go' for a while. If your children are ill, don't be over-concerned about the housework. If you are bogged down with work, cook convenience foods for a week. Be realistic; neglecting some areas for a short time won't result in a total collapse of your lifestyle, and when times are hard don't make them even harder for yourself by trying to maintain unnecessary standards.

4. Learn to recognise stress in yourself

In order to deal effectively with stress you need to recognise those times when the pressure is building, so that you can take action before the stress reaches a level you feel unable to cope with. Write yourself an action plan and learn to be prompt about putting it into effect. You don't need to sit by feeling helpless, while the pressure builds.

5. Ways to relieve stress

Find a positive and effective method of relieving stress that works for you and then *use* it. Below are some ideas of what you could do.

◆ Relaxation exercises

◆ Take up an active sport

◆ An absorbing and relaxing hobby e.g. painting

◆ A long soak in the bath with a glass of wine

◆ A night out with the girls

- ◆ A weekend break
- ◆ Golden moments (create a short stress-free ritual, e.g. a cup of coffee and the crossword, stopping the car on the way home from work to listen to music, a brief focus on the beauty of nature etc.)

Dealing with a stressful relationship

Being embroiled in a stressful relationship is very debilitating and can lead you to become negative about your life. Determine now that you will find an effective way of dealing with it and don't be willing to endure it for whatever reason. Even if this relationship can never be perfect, it can be improved and less cause for stress. The following suggestions may help you tackle this problem.

① Have courage. If this is a problem you are nervous of tackling, hang on to the thought that if the final outcome is an improvement, it is worth some anguish.

② Find ways of talking calmly and constructively to the other person involved. If necessary arrange a 'meeting' when you will not be disturbed, with an 'agenda'. Draw up ground rules of behaviour which you must both adhere to, e.g. no interrupting, no put-downs, no personal attacks, etc. If you think this sounds too 'over the top', stop and consider that if it succeeds where other attempts have failed then it is worth-while.

③ Ask someone impartial to act as mediator. This can help both parties involved 'behave' properly and the mediator can be objective about the situation.

④ Seek advice from friends or professionals. Someone else may offer a new insight or a fresh approach that is worth consideration.

⑤ Examine your own attitude and honestly consider if some of your negative views could be changed or if you need to be more flexible and tolerant.

Twelve ways to stress-proof yourself

At times of crises, for example when someone suddenly 'has a go' at you, you can learn to use an emergency coping strategy to prevent the stress response from being activated or to lessen its effect.

♦ Don't panic – breathe deeply for a short time or count slowly to ten.

♦ Tell yourself to keep calm.

♦ Decide to deal with a problem later, once your emotions have calmed down.

♦ Look for the funny side of a situation.

♦ Set a time deadline when you will stop thinking about a problem.

♦ Look for reasons behind other people's actions.

♦ Take a check on your priorities.

♦ Step outside the situation and take an objective look.

♦ Ask the other person involved if you can both take time to reflect and resume discussion afterwards.

♦ Don't get locked into a spiral of conflict, find a way of removing yourself.

♦ Practise a ten minute relaxation technique.

♦ Write down five rational and positive statements about a situation.

What women told us

Sue: *'I see my work piling up and I'm filled with panic.'*
Jill: *'I've lost the art of relaxing; being constantly busy has become a way of life.'*
Annie: *'As far as I'm concerned, exhaustion is the norm.'*

Molly's story

I know I'm stressed because I'm always tired and have frequent headaches, but I cannot see a way of relieving the pressures. Everything seems of paramount importance and I just don't know what I could drop or put onto someone else. It really worries me at times that I might crack up but I still carry on regardless.

Energy is the key to a happier life

Revitalise your energy wells

Many working mothers have little if any time that they devote entirely to themselves. Yet if they want to cope effectively with stress and lead happy and fulfilled lives, they must ensure that their own reserves are not depleted. Fulfilling your own needs is vital if you are to cater successfully for other people. The following diagram illustrates those areas in your life that need to be revitalised from time to time. We have coined the phrase 'wells' as this image aptly conveys their refreshing potential.

Emotional Well
Make time to have fun and enjoy the company of others. Learn to express feelings, talk over problems, build loving supportive relationships.

Spiritual Well
Revitalise your sense of wonderment and awe. You may find this in religious beliefs, from meditation or contemplating nature.

Cognitive Well
Replenish this well by reading books, watching plays/films, debating ideas, making plans, thinking things through, doing crossword puzzles, etc.

Creative Well
Appreciate art, take up creative hobbies, dance, sing, make exciting recipes, etc.

Physical Well
Get adequate rest, take regular physical exercise, eat a healthy diet, practise relaxation techniques, go for a massage.

You

I will try and replenish my 'wells' by doing the following:

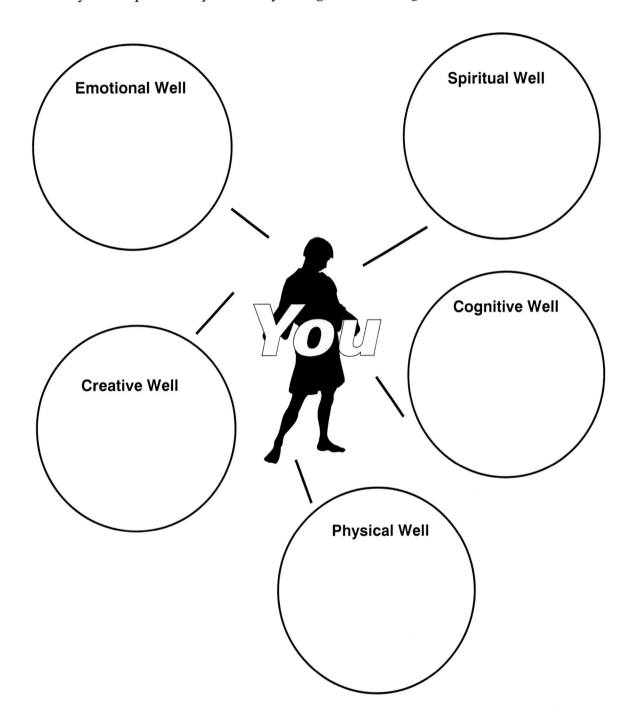

Set aside a regular weekly slot of time when you can re-charge your batteries by doing something you have chosen just for your pleasure and enjoyment. Also, try writing a weekly care plan with some small treat or opportunity for enjoyment each day.

	For week commencing Sunday 3rd November
Sunday	Spend ½ hour on hair giving it a special conditioning treatment
Monday	Ring my friend Mary and catch up on all her gossip
Tuesday	Have a long, luxurious soak in the bath with fragrant bath oils
Wednesday	Buy a magazine and read it all
Thursday	Treat myself to a meal out with friends
Friday	Have an early night with a good book
Saturday	Make time for a swim with the children

Combat negative thinking

When everything seems to be going wrong and you're feeling helpless and hopeless, it will help you to regain an equilibrium in your life if you can replace your negative thoughts with more positive ones. The following ideas may be useful in starting this process.

Don't overlook what is positive

When we're feeling 'down' we tend to focus only on all the bad things that happen, which reinforces how we feel. Usually this is a very lopsided view of our lives, so next time you are feeling low take the trouble to write down all the good and positive things that occur to try and bring a realistic balance back.

All the positive things that have happened today
A letter arrived from my friend abroad
The sun was shining
The boss thanked me for reminding her to take the folder of additional information

You can use this same process when you are feeling particularly low about yourself. Write down all the qualities and skills you do possess or, better still, ask your friends to do this for you. It can be a real boost to know that other people recognise and appreciate positive things about you.

My qualities	My skills
Patient	Good at budgeting
Kind	Good organiser
Thorough	Good listener

Balance your weaknesses with strengths

When you are feeling particularly vulnerable about your weaknesses, it may help to consider that often people's strengths and weaknesses are the reverse sides of the same coin. Try and find the strength that balances your weakness. It does not mean that you should not try and improve your areas of weakness, but it may help put them in perspective and make you feel less negative.

Examples

Weakness	Strength
'I'm so disorganised about housework.'	'I have great spontaneity for creating fun occasions.'
'I'm overly fussy about manners.'	'People often comment on how polite and well behaved my children are.'

Now fill in the boxes about yourself.

Weakness	Strength

Change your perspective

The way in which you view yourself, others or situations will influence your feelings and responses. The following scenarios give examples of this.

Abby's story

As a child Abby was frequently told that she was thoughtless and selfish, and still believes this is basically true. She has had a particularly busy time with her family and forgot to send a Mother's Day card. When she realises this she is immediately filled with horror and self-loathing that she can have done something so thoughtless and selfish. She spends lots of time berating herself, feels really miserable, sends a huge bouquet of flowers she can ill afford to her mother and suffers pangs of guilt for weeks afterwards.

Nina's story

Nina, who was generally told she was kind and considerate as a child, has also forgotten Mother's Day. When she realises this fact she telephones her mother, apologises, explains the circumstances that caused her to forget, expresses her love for her mother, then forgets the incident.

The difference between Abby and Nina is that Abby has, entrenched in her self-image, the belief that she is selfish and thoughtless. She does not consider that she has always remembered Mother's Day on previous occasions or that circumstances caused her to forget. She only sees that the view of herself as a thoughtless, selfish person has once again been confirmed. She has lost the true perspective of the incident, in a negative self-belief. Abby is no more selfish than Nina, the difference lies in their respective self-images.

Negative comments that have been made to you by other people are based on their expectations and values. This does not make them necessarily true. Think of some of the negative beliefs you have about yourself and which cause you guilt, write them down in the boxes on the next page and see if you can challenge them.

Examples:

Negative self-belief	My challenge
I'm sloppy and messy	When I look around, I don't seem much worse than anyone else. I might not meet my mother's standards of cleanliness and hygiene, but my home does not present a health hazard and everyone else accepts me as I am.
I'm self-centred	I do lead a very busy life and can be forgetful, but I do actually think a lot about others and try to remember important events in other peoples lives. If I do forget I make amends in my own way.

Now fill in three of your negative self-beliefs and your challenge.

Negative self-belief	My challenge

You can also try this procedure to change your perspective of other people or situations. If you can view them in a more positive light your feelings and responses will improve accordingly.

Be your own friend

Many people judge themselves much more harshly than they would others. You might point out to a friend the areas in her life where she 'brings trouble on herself' and offer sound advice that is constructive and helpful, but you would not condemn her as someone who is not worthwhile or of no value. Try and be your own friend when you are feeling worthless and instead of condemning your behaviour give yourself the sort of good advice you would offer to a friend.

Accept failure as part of life

When things go wrong and you or other people make mistakes or fail, try and accept this as a natural aspect of human existence. Failure is a normal part of any learning process and the more tolerant you can be with yourself the greater tolerance you will have for others.

In this chapter, you have considered many aspects of your dual roles as worker and mother. By now you should have a more complete and realistic picture of yourself and ideas of how you could make positive changes in your life. You are now going to write out an action plan to deal with one of these areas of change. You might think that making an action plan is a waste of time, since you have already determined the change and thought of how you intend to proceed, but writing it all down is in fact a very helpful process. The following pointers explain why.

♦ Writing things down helps to clarify your aims and objectives.

♦ Filling in a chart provides you with the facts of your progress (if you are on a high you tend to remember only the successes and if you are feeling low you tend to focus on failures.)

♦ Displaying your action plan somewhere prominent acts as a constant reminder.

Before writing your action plan there are certain considerations that you need to take into account.

Consider all the aspects

Make sure you fully understand all the aspects involved in any change you want to make and consider all the factors that might affect your success, such as:

♦ Does your lifestyle allow you sufficient time to work on your action plan?

♦ Do you need to enlist the support and cooperation of others?

♦ Do you need to change your own views and behaviours?

Set a realistic target

Your ultimate goal may seem too far off and daunting for you to tackle. If this is the case, break it down into smaller steps. Start with a more realistic target and progress from there each time you succeed.

Example:

You want to improve your relationship with your partner's mother who lives with you, but this blanket statement seems too big to encompass. You might therefore progress through the following steps.

1 Set aside 5–10 minutes uninterrupted time each day, when you will talk about something positive with her (avoid any topics or issues that might lead to confrontation.)

2 Plan together an outing or treat you will both enjoy.

3 When you are both in a positive frame of mind, work out together a system whereby you can calmly discuss issues of concern.

4 Practise using this system on a fairly small issue to see how it works and if it needs modification.

5 When you feel ready, tackle a larger more controversial issue.

Give yourself/others a reward

Rewards are a very important part of success. We all like to have our efforts acknowledged and applauded, so think of a suitable reward for yourself (and others if they have helped in effecting change) for when you have achieved your target. It could be a meal out with your partner, a visit to the hairdressers, a family celebration – anything that you feel will give you a well-deserved pat on the back.

Be prepared for setbacks

Don't allow setbacks to demoralise you and cause you to give up. You have to be realistic and understand that changing patterns of behaviour or circumstances is often a huge undertaking. If you are trying to change aspects of yourself, then you are beginning a new learning process and you must remember that all learning involves steps forward, plateaux and occasional steps back. Try to discover what caused the setback and look at it realistically and objectively. If, however, you continue to fail to reach your target, don't just give up. Re-think your target and consider the following:

1 Does the target need to be modified to make it more achievable?

2 Have I really understood the changes that need to be made?

How to write your action plan

Having considered all the elements of an action plan you can now think about writing your own. Concentrate on one area at a time and start with the areas that you think will be easier to deal with. Read through the two examples below.

Example 1:   **At home**

Area I would like to see change	How I feel
I'm too shy to talk to other mums at school functions, but I'd really like to have one or two friendly acquaintances.	I can't think of anything to say to them, I'm hopeless at small talk. I feel panicky and boring.
What I could do	**Target**
Write out and rehearse some conversations. Ask Sam who his special friends are and talk to their mothers.	To be on friendly terms with one or two mothers so I don't always feel an outsider at school functions. To invite a mother and her son to tea one day.
Reward	**Setbacks**
I'll treat myself to a bath luxury every time I have a conversation with another mother.	I did speak to one mother but then froze up and couldn't talk to another. *Cause* Sudden loss of confidence.
Way Forward	
I know I can do it if I really persevere. I must keep on reminding myself of the future benefits to myself and Sam.	

Area I would like to see change	How I feel
I keep missing Rosie's school events. She gets so upset with me.	I feel really guilty that I'm so neglectful. I just can't remember beforehand to arrange for time off work.
What I could do	**Target**
Put up a big noticeboard in my kitchen. Each time I get notice of a forthcoming event I'll write out in big letters the event and date and pin it to the board so I see it every day.	To get through half a term without missing anything.
Reward	**Setbacks**
Every time I attend an event, Rosie will stick a star onto a piece of card for me. If I don't miss any, she will make me a 'Best Mum in the World' badge.	Missed one event. *Cause* I had an important meeting which I had to attend.
Way Forward	
As long as I make the effort to be at most events, Rosie will try and understand that sometimes work has to come first.	

Fill in the following two charts, each with one area of your life at home that you have decided to work on.

Area I would like to see change	How I feel
What I could do	**Target**
Reward	**Setbacks**
	Cause
Way Forward	

Area I would like to see change	How I feel
What I could do	**Target**
Reward	**Setbacks**
	Cause
Way Forward	

You can also use Action Plans to help with areas of concern you may have at work.

Example 1:   **At work**

Area I would like to see change	How I feel
I keep having to ask colleagues at work to help me sort out my computer problems.	Unprofessional and guilty.
What I could do	**Target**
Take advantage of some of the courses provided by my company.	To take regular computing courses in order to gain more skills.
Reward	**Setbacks**
I'll treat myself to a plant for my room each time I complete a course.	None so far. *Cause*
Way Forward	
To make sure I keep practising the new skills I have learned.	

Example 2:

Area I would like to see change	How I feel
I'm scared stiff of the senior partner.	Terrified in case he talks to me.
What I could do	**Target**
Write out and practise small pleasantries I could say to him.	To be able to converse naturally with him.
Reward	**Setbacks**
An aromatherapy massage.	I chickened out a couple of times. *Cause* Sheer terror, lack of confidence.
Way Forward	
I mean to keep to this plan of action until I feel confident enough to stop avoiding him.	

Fill in the following two charts, each with one area of your life at work that you have decided to work on.

Area I would like to see change	How I feel
What I could do	**Target**
Reward	**Setbacks**
	Cause
Way Forward	

Area I would like to see change	How I feel

What I could do	Target

Reward	Setbacks
	Cause

Way Forward

Are you striking the right balance in your life?

Having completed the previous action plans to improve your home and work life, you need now to explore whether you are achieving a happy balance between them. Finding that elusive balance between career and family life is not easy. We all read about superwomen who juggle with glittering careers, raise families of bright, engaging children, entertain large numbers of people at the drop of a hat in their immaculate homes, are the perfect lover for their adoring, dynamic partners, and practise fencing and glass-blowing in their spare times. It may please you to learn that none of the working mothers whom we talked to were anything like this! Working motherhood for most of us is incredibly hard work which requires constant, daily appraisal. With so much going on and so many demands on your time and attention, it is easy to get off balance and put all your energy into work or family or other commitments. Much juggling is required to balance your life in order to give appropriate weight to your professional life, your family and other relationships and yourself.

♦ Giving time to your work means putting time aside for your own career development as well as giving time and energy to your current job. Does your work suffer because family concerns take a disproportionate amount of your time?

♦ Giving time to developing relationships with others may mean choosing to put less time and energy into your work. Do you spend enough time building relationships with the important people in your life, your partner, children, parents friends and colleagues?

♦ Giving time to yourself includes taking care of your health, and your mental and spiritual development. Do you neglect your own wants and needs in the rush of your everyday life?

Look through the statements on the following page and mark the appropriate box.

	Agree	Disagree
I find time to relax each week without feeling guilty	☐	☐
I enjoy a good social life	☐	☐
Work commitments don't encroach on my time at home	☐	☐
I have enough energy left for evening activities with my family	☐	☐
I make a point of phoning and writing to friends and family to keep in touch	☐	☐
I don't often disappoint my family because of sudden extra work commitments	☐	☐
Working does not place any real pressure on my relationships with members of my family	☐	☐
I keep my professional aspirations alive by giving attention to my career development	☐	☐
I enjoy being with my family as much as I enjoy being at work	☐	☐
I make time to see my friends	☐	☐
I feel comfortable with the division of time between home and work	☐	☐
I make time to exercise regularly	☐	☐
I set aside time to spend on my own interests regularly	☐	☐
I am able to fulfil my work role satisfactorily	☐	☐
I don't often neglect work commitments because of family needs/demands	☐	☐
I make time to build good relationships with people at work	☐	☐
I usually try to attend social functions at work	☐	☐

If your life was ideally balanced between your work, your family and friends and yourself, a circular chart showing this perfect balance might look something like this:

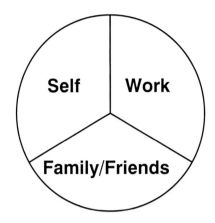

Consider the balance in the lives of some of the working mothers described below. Draw lines to indicate what you think the graph of the person described would look like. What percentage of the mother's life would be devoted to work, self and relationships with family and friends?

Sally has a demanding job as a buyer.
She usually works on Saturday.
She exercises regularly in the gym, goes jogging in the evening when she feels stressed.
She is a very keen gardener.
Her daughter is often asleep by the time she gets home in the evening.

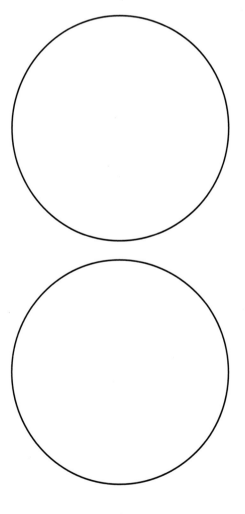

Joan is a single mother with three children aged 5, 6 and11. She works full-time for a finance company.
She manages to pick up her children from school each day but has to bring home work each evening in order to make sure she keeps up with the work.

Jill has 2 children, one of whom is at school.
She works part-time as a secretary. One of her children is diabetic and needs to have regular medical check-ups. Her husband was made redundant last year so money is a worry.

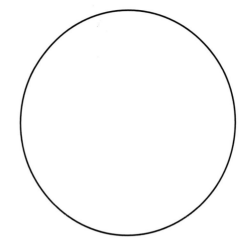

How balanced is your life?

Make a graph for yourself in the circle provided.

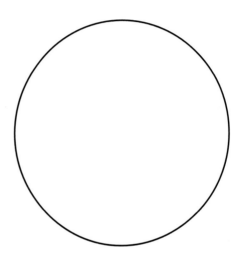

How much time and energy do you give to your work?

The next short questionnaire will help you to think about the time and energy you currently invest in your work, and consider whether this is a necessary or chosen relationship. If you are not employed at present, or if you are working from home, imagine how you would react.

(Mark the letter against the sentence that applies to you.)

Situation 1

It is 11am. Your boss has asked you if you would be prepared to work two hours later that evening to finish some important work for her. You have friends coming for supper whom you invited a month ago.

Would you:

(a) Tell her that it is impossible for you to do this as you have a long-standing engagement that can't be changed.

(b) Tell her that you cannot stay late but suggest that you are prepared to work through your lunch hour.

(c) Tell her that you can manage one hour after work (by arranging to have friends arrive later than planned) and/or work through your lunch hour.

(d) Work the extra time and buy a take-away for your friends.

(e) Cancel your friends visit and work the extra time.

Situation 2

Your child is whining that he does not want to go to the babyminder and when you arrive says he has tummy ache and feels sick. The babyminder is very kind and capable.

Do you:

(a) Ring work and say that you won't be in today, without much hesitation.

(b) Ring up to explain the circumstances, hoping to negotiate time off.

(c) Go to work and ring home frequently to see how things are. Spend the day not really being able to concentrate fully on the task in hand.

(d) Go to work and manage to concentrate on your job for the most part although your thoughts wander to home some of the time.

(e) Go to work and have the self-discipline to block home from your mind completely so that you are able to cope as well as you do normally.

Situation 3

You have a work task to complete in a week's time and you know you could do a much better job by putting in extra hours at home.

Do you:

(a) Have no desire to do more than is possible in the time you have available at work.

(b) Feel annoyed that you can't do the job as well as you might, but do no extra work at home.

(c) Spend extra time at home improving the work, but make sure it doesn't intrude on non-work activities.

(d) Spend long evenings at the task but take some time off at the weekend for a break.

(e) Spend all the hours you need to give this task top priority over anything you have planned at home.

Situation 4

Friends suggest an impromptu one-week holiday to start in less than two weeks time. You can afford the holiday, and the children can accompany you. You are ready for the break and have the holiday due to you and it will not inconvenience others at work. However, you have a very interesting week ahead – entertaining/conferences (or other work activities you enjoy that would be appropriate in your case). Many important people will attend the conference.

Do you:

(a) Inform your employer of your plans, book up and go off with your friends without a moment's hesitation.

(b) Say you will go and try to rearrange some of the work activities and cancel others.

(c) Tell your friends that you are unable to take the time off work but try to persuade them to take a later holiday that is more convenient for you.

(d) Say you are unable to go but feel rather disappointed that you will miss out on the holiday.

(e) Say you are unable to go and recognise that the decision was not a difficult one to make.

Situation 5

You are offered a promotion that will involve your being away from home for two nights a week. You know that your partner/parents is/are willing to take responsibility for your commitments on these occasions and would encourage you to take the promotion.

Do you:

(a) Turn down the offer without any hesitation?

(b) Consider the offer briefly but know it isn't for you?

(c) Spend ages thinking what to do and planning how you could manage to take the promotion without your home life being affected unduly?

(d) Accept the job with a few misgivings, but recognise that this promotion is what you want?

(e) Accept the promotion right away with real enthusiasm and no feeling or conflict?

You have considered the amount of time and energy that you are prepared to invest in your work in different situations. Using your results as a guide see whether or not you can identify the category that best describes you.

 A's Your family commitments, personal life and social activities always come first for you and your role as home-maker is what matters. You are not fully investing your energy and interest in your career. The type of work with which you are occupied is possibly not of real significance. As long as it is convenient, fairly interesting with a friendly work atmosphere, and provides you with enough money to pay for your main requirements and some extras, you are happy. It is important for you to have a job that does not intrude on your personal and social activities and responsibilities. You are unlikely to seek promotion and would only accept changes that fitted in easily with your home responsibilities and social life. You are probably employed in a work situation where you could do the job 'standing on your head'.

B's You are prepared to work reasonably hard and you enjoy interesting work. You have probably been careful to select work that you can cope with fairly easily but that does provide you with some challenges and variety. However you want to have a 9–5 job where 5pm means 5pm! You are not prepared to let work intrude into your personal life/home life, which is your first priority. You would be prepared to accept promotion but only on your terms, so it is unlikely that you would be prepared to travel away from home or take a job that entailed working at the weekends. You rely on others to prompt you into considering a career change or retraining to develop your talents. It is likely that you are working in a job that is under-using your skills at present.

C's Your work is important to you. You put real effort into your job and seek work that is interesting and stimulating. You are conscientious and keen to make progress and actively seek promotion and change. However, because your home life/social activities are as important to you as your work, you often find yourself in stressful situations trying to juggle home, family and work and attempting to do *everything*. You are constantly feeling pressurised by events and feel you don't achieve as well as you could do in either role.

D's Your work is extremely important to you and certainly takes precedence over your leisure activities and home commitments. You have worked conscientiously to achieve your present role and are always ready to consider promotion and change. If this involves weekend work, or time away from home, you would organise family and friends to accommodate this. You are fairly ruthless in the pursuit of your goals and although you enjoy your social activities you let people know that work comes first with you. You need to have interesting, varied work with good promotion prospects and you spend time thinking about your next move. Your general happiness in life depends on how you feel about your achievements in work.

E's There is really no distinction between your work and your leisure activities. You enjoy your work so much, and it is so central to your life, that you would be happy with relatively few family and social commitments. Family and friends sometimes accuse you of being too involved in your work. You couldn't possibly work in a situation where you didn't feel totally committed and absorbed. You are prepared to give up most things in pursuit of your goals, working long hours, weekends, travelling away from home would present few difficulties for you. Your happiness in life is closely related to your self-esteem and progress at work.

Is your work taking up too much of your time and energy?

Do you feel your life is out of balance because of work commitments?

The pressure of having more work than you can handle on a regular basis can lead to stress at home and at work. You may find you are suffering headaches, tiredness, irritability, sleeping difficulties, nausea, nervousness or other warning signs that you are under pressure. You may be a person who is not easily stressed by overload but worry that your relationship with the children, family and friends is suffering because of work commitments. All relationships need nurturing if they are to grow and flourish. If work demands leave you with little time and energy for your family and friends these relationships may deteriorate as you lose out on precious time together. Unfortunately, people can be unaware that this is happening until a crisis occurs that shocks them into realising that they have not been as close to people as they had thought. It is important to recognise the warning signs and take action. Find different ways of coping with the workload and ways of easing the pressure for yourself at work and at home.

Behave more assertively

Learning to behave more assertively at work is essential if you want to avoid work taking over all of your life. Although you cannot do anything to change the nature of a demanding boss or thoughtless colleagues, you will, with practice, be able to restrict their impact on your job and life. Assertive behaviour relies on discussion, negotiation and compromise; it involves expressing yourself directly and honestly without feeling afraid or anxious. As you learn to behave assertively, you will gradually abandon passive, manipulative or aggressive interactions, because assertiveness works much better and allows you to feel in control and happier with yourself.

Learn to say 'no' to additional work commitments

If you often find yourself working extra hours or bringing work home that you hadn't bargained for, is it because you find it difficult to say 'no'? If these tasks are outside your contracted working hours and agreed obligations, what makes it difficult for you to refuse them? Saying 'no' is probably one of the most difficult words to say and usually stems from the beliefs we hold.

Do you say 'yes' when you want to say 'no' because:

♦ You don't want to displease the other person

♦ You don't feel you can let colleagues down

♦ You do it to earn the gratitude and respect of others.

♦ You're frightened of the consequences of saying 'no'

71

- You think you won't be promoted

- You enjoy being thought of as someone who is always ready and willing to 'go the extra mile'

- You think other people's needs are more important than yours

If any of these statements are true for you, you will be led to say 'yes' when you want to say 'no'. If you do take on extra work, stay late, change your days off, or say 'yes' unhappily to other requests, you may find yourself not only overworked, but resentful towards your boss, crabby with your family, and annoyed with yourself. If you want to say 'no', it is vital to change your belief to one which holds that *other people have the right to ask things of me, but I have the right to refuse.* Unless your contract or agreement has specified otherwise you are under no obligation to take on extra work and are perfectly within your rights to refuse to do so. You may be thinking at this point that there are certain requests that you cannot refuse to carry out, even though they are not strictly in your contract. Obviously, you might want to help out in times of crisis, to complete something important, or because it is expedient to do so, but do not allow taking on additional work to become the rule rather than the exception. If you help out in this way, it is important that you make clear the difficulties that will arise for you in complying with the request: 'I will get the report done for Thursday though this will mean putting off the Monday meeting for a couple of days,' or 'I will work late on Friday, though this will involve rearranging times with the childminder.'

Guidelines for saying 'no'

Notice your reaction and trust it

Your body will let you know whether you feel like agreeing or refusing (a certain sinking feeling in the stomach will be evident).

Give yourself time

If you find yourself hesitating say 'Could you give me some time to think about it?' or 'Could you tell me something more about it?'

Keep the reply short (but not abrupt)

Don't use long-winded sentences filled with excuses and apologies, e.g. 'Well I'm not really sure about Wednesday, I don't think that's a good day for the babyminder to have Alex after 5pm and I'm not sure if my car will be back from the garage by then and ...'

Give the real reason for refusing

Don't invent an excuse – it makes you feel guilty and is often recognised as such by the other person.

Practise saying 'no' at the beginning of the statement

'No, I won't be able to stay late on Wednesday ...'
'No, I'm not happy to take on the job of writing the minutes ...'

'No, I prefer to use the computer I'm used to.'

This is far better than a flimsy excuse or changing your mind later, having initially agreed to do something for another person.

Do not hover around after you have said 'no'

This only encourages the other person to try to change your mind.

Do acknowledge your own feelings

'I find it difficult to say no.'

'I feel ungrateful for having to refuse.'

Ask how they feel, and if possible offer an alternative

Sometimes people may be hurt, feel rejected or annoyed by your refusal but remember you are refusing the request, not rejecting the person.

You may feel guilty for refusing requests assertively at first but it will get easier with practice. The benefits from being able to say 'no' clearly, directly and honestly include:

♦ having more time to spend on things you want to say 'yes' to

♦ people trusting you to say what you mean

♦ feeling happier and more confident about making decisions

♦ people respecting the decisions you make

♦ having more self-respect

Streamline your work

Are there areas of your work that you could streamline and make more efficient or less time-consuming, to reduce the incidence of extra work commitments? Look through the following ideas to see if any could be applied to help you.

Daily To-do list Spend some time each day looking through work and make a 'To - do' list prioritising your jobs from most to least important. This way you won't reach the end of the day and realise you have not completed the most urgent task.

Cut the distractions You might well be surprised by the frequency and amount of times you are distracted from your tasks. Try filling in the chart below to obtain a realistic idea of the time lost in distractions. Include everything e.g. phone calls, conversations with colleagues, customers etc., daydreaming, reading anything unrelated, not being able to locate necessary items . *Don't cheat* by cutting short conversations etc. just because you know you are writing the distractions down – behave as normal.

Distraction	Time lost from task

Were you shocked by the time wasted in distractions? Devise strategies to reduce these, e.g. don't keep tempting magazines on your desk. Use a timer for conversations when you know you might be drawn into time-wasting chit-chat: set the timer for 10 minutes to remind you just how long you've been talking.

Cut down on unnecessary details

Look at how you work to see if you are aiming for perfection by spending too much time worrying over unnecessary details, e.g. in presentation, in considering all aspects. Learn not to be over-fussy about details that aren't really relevant or important.

Tackling big or boring tasks

If you have to tackle a big or boring task you are likely to be more easily distracted or less able to concentrate efficiently. Is it possible to break down the task into smaller chunks and do a little each day?

Keep paperwork to a minimum Make a list of all the paperwork you attend to in a day/week. Read through the list to see if all the paperwork is necessary, otherwise you are (a) wasting time filling things in and (b) creating extra material to be filed or read through. Cut paperwork down to only what is essential.

Throw away junk mail Don't waste time reading through irrelevant mail. A quick glance should tell you whether it is relevant or not. Be ruthless about immediately consigning everything else to the waste paper bin.

List of instructions and procedures It's a good idea for your company to have lists of instructions, e.g. for using machines and work procedures. This cuts down on time wasted in telling others what to do and how to go about things.

Useful crisis list Compile a list of useful names and telephone numbers for crises, e.g. when machines break down or problems arise. This can cut down on time spent trying to find the relevant contracts.

Estimate the amount of time jobs will take Try and get into the habit of estimating how long each task will take you. This can be helpful in encouraging you to keep to the time you've decided on and not to take on more than you can comfortably handle in a day.

Organise work materials Make sure that all the materials you need are easily accessible and well organised. Hunting for things you need can be frustrating and take up unnecessary time.

Meetings Don't attend meetings just for the sake of putting in an appearance. If any are unnecessary or irrelevant, give them a miss.

Time of day Try and schedule exacting tasks for when you are fresh and better able to concentrate. Save the more mundane and routine jobs for those times of the day when fatigue limits your ability to 'get to grips' with anything too demanding.

Long-term projects If you have any long-term, non-essential projects, draw up an action plan breaking them down into smaller chunks. You can then tackle each section when time allows. This can be very helpful if the overall project is going to take a considerable time and you are likely to continually defer it, because of this.

Example:
Your company wants you to find a way of interesting more local clients in your product.

Action Plan	Time allowed
1 Look through selection of adverts – jot down useful or eye-catching ideas	2 hours
2 Roughly draft a flier advertising product to show boss, colleagues etc.	1½–2 hours
3 Refine rough draft for printing	2 hours
4 Make a list of suitable local companies	2–3 hours
5 Send off fliers to companies	1½ hours

Try writing an action plan for one of your long term projects, breaking it down into more manageable chunks of time which you will be able to fit in to your present work schedule.

Action Plan	Time allowed

Saving energy at work Try and make sure that you organise your time efficiently so that you don't waste energy. For example, don't make two journeys to the same place when more efficient organisation would mean you only have to make one journey. Try and streamline any tasks that duplicate your efforts and waste unnecessary energy.

Make decisions Don't allow decision-making to take up too much time. If you know that you spend far too long procrastinating, find ways of reducing this. Write out pros and cons and other helpful information if this would help or set yourself a deadline for making up your mind and stick to it.

Recap

Hopefully, you now have some ideas about how you could streamline your work in order to save time and use it more efficiently. However, it is up to you to put these ideas into practice. They might need some effort and initiative to put into place, but this could be well rewarded in future benefit to you.

Work fulfilling needs

If you still find that work commitments occupy most of your waking life, perhaps you have unconsciously allowed this to happen. If this is the case you should consider what needs your work is fulfilling that are not being met elsewhere. Look through the following reasons to see if any apply to you.

◆ Does your work offer you respect and a boost to your self-esteem that you do not receive elsewhere?

◆ Does your work provide the sort of interest that eclipses the humdrum existence of your home life?

◆ Does work provide an escape route from unhappy or unsatisfying relationships at home?

◆ Have you become addicted to a high-finance lifestyle and need to work long hours to provide the income you need to finance this?

Whatever your reasons, if you have become or are in danger of becoming a workaholic you need to understand and consider the cost factors.

All work and no play

Remember the old saying 'All work and no play makes Jack a dull boy'. Have you become overly occupied with and intense about work, leaving little time for fun, relaxation or other interests? If so, you are in a situation that is not conducive to long-term health or happiness. Working too intensively can lead to exhaustion and 'burn out', where both your body and your mind are more vulnerable to infections and disorders. Moreover, your 'wholeness' as a person will become less complete as work-centred activity narrows and confines your horizons. If your world shrinks to just work and very little else, you will be missing out on all the other possibilities that life could offer you.

Establish priorities

We all have our own list of priorities based on the values we hold, external pressures, other people's expectations, time and resources available etc. The set of priorities we have will not be the same as our partner's, friends', children's or colleagues'. In fact, because priorities are personal to each individual they can be very different and at times, conflicting. This is especially true, when one's priorities become rigid and inflexible as is illustrated in the following scenario.

Alice's story

One of Alice's most important priorities has been that Sunday should be sacrosanct as a family day. She, her husband and her children look forward to and enjoy this time they spend together. A major crisis has occurred at work because an order for an important client has been bungled and the client is threatening to take his business elsewhere. Alice's boss asks her to work with him on the following day (Sunday) in order to rectify the mistake, placate the client and not lose future business. Alice feels that she only has one day a week with her family and they are entitled to this consideration, so refuses her boss's request.

It would not have been unreasonable for Alice to have put her loyalty to work before her loyalty to her family on this occasion, but her priorities have become rigidly fixed with no room for manoeuvre or compromise. When this happens, it can lead to lack of accommodation to the needs of others.

Tackling the urgent

Being more flexible with your priorities means that you can evaluate them continually and if necessary change them, either temporarily or permanently. It is very tempting to always deal with what seems most urgent at a cost sometimes of what is more important. An example of this follows.

Marijka's story

Marijka wants to finish a report for work. Her teenage daughter, obviously upset, wants to talk to her. Marijka tells her they will talk, when she has completed the report. However, when the report is finished, Marijka discovers that her daughter has left the house without informing her of her whereabouts. Marijka is now very anxious for her daughter's well-being.

Of course, it is not always easy or straightforward to evaluate which priority is most important, but at least you should try and be aware that it may not necessarily be what seems most urgent.

Allow for spontaneity

Some types of priority really kill unexpected opportunities if they become too rigidly maintained, e.g. 'I believe children need a well-ordered lifestyle. My kids always eat at 4.30pm and go to bed at 7.30pm.' You and your children could miss out on all sorts of spontaneous opportunities for fun and enjoyment if this type of priority was strenuously adhered to.

Make a list of your priorities at home and at work and go through the following steps.

♦ Re-evaluate how important they are

♦ Consider if they have become too rigid and need to be made more feasible

♦ Discuss with other people how to find accommodating solutions when your priorities clash with theirs

♦ Be prepared to juggle your priorities if an occasion calls for this

My home priorities	My comments about them

My home priorities	My comments about them

My work priorities	My comments about them

Strengthen your support

A network of people you can turn to for emotional and practical support takes away some of the stress and panic when you are feeling overwhelmed with your work. Involve a range of people in your support network, from like-minded friends to neighbours, work colleagues and additional babyminders or nannies whom you can ask to help out in an emergency. The working mothers you meet when you have your baby often prove to be particularly valuable since they may share similar concerns and commitments.

> ## Anna's story
>
> With my first two children I had a colleague at work who had a job like mine with children in the same class at the local school. It was great because we always took each other's children at a moment's notice. When her mother was ill, I had her children for a week and felt able to leave mine with her when I had to travel for work. I have a young baby now and haven't yet found this type of relationship with a friend and I miss the comfort of knowing that there is someone always willing to help out no matter what.

Support groups

If you haven't support of this kind, contact other working mothers in your organisation to see if you can build a support group to share experiences and needs and find practical way of working together for mutual benefit. The more people you know in a similar situation, the easier it is to build up additional support networks for such things as sharing transport and childcare. A working mother's group can act as a force for change by putting forward ideas to management about the needs of working mothers, presenting proposals which have been successful in other organisations, organising summer holiday schemes for school age children and providing a contact point for part-time workers, women returners or those mothers on maternity leave.

Sharing personal experiences and concerns with other working mothers is a real bonus, helping you to see things in perspective and substantially reduce the stress in your life. If joining or initiating a support group is not possible in your organisation, do seek out other local groups such as Working Mothers groups, NCT groups, babysitting groups, pre-school groups, or the PTA, who are always pleased to have additional members. Do actively seek ways of helping out other women in the group whenever you get the opportunity and you will find it easier to ask for their help when you need it. These favours might be offering to collect or take someone's child to school with yours, inviting a child to stay overnight, freeing someone for the whole day, looking after neighbours' children at the weekend. Most mothers appreciate a time to themselves occasionally and will be keen to take up your offer!

Neighbours

Supportive neighbours are extremely valuable. It is worth putting time and effort into developing a friendly relationship with them, especially if they like and welcome children. It can save hours of stress for everyone on those occasions when you can't get back to let your child in, find yourself locked out or get a phone call to say that your child has lost or forgotten his key. A friendly neighbour can also be a godsend for letting in delivery men, helping out in emergencies when cars won't start or children are ill. Make sure you offer services in kind which may include, for those without children, watering the garden or looking after pets or getting shopping for them.

Surrogate grannies

Some working mothers with no family nearby, advertise for an older person to act as a grandma to the children. If you decide to take this step, you need to consider carefully whether you are willing to make a commitment to helping the older person practically and emotionally. There will be real benefits for the children if the relationship works well and you may find you get help when the children are ill, with babysitting, as well as an enthusiastic games player and story-reader.

Childminders and nannies

The most important support for many working mothers is that provided by their childminder or nanny. Since your child may spend many hours a week in her care, it is important for your peace of mind that her approach is as similar as possible to yours. Where a single individual is to care for your child, it will be helpful to think about and discuss in advance with her, preferably on a visit to her home, issues that may concern you. These might be concerns about food, mealtimes, discipline, toilet training, sleeping and so on. If you are employing a nanny or au-pair it is a good idea to write out a contract stating terms of employment and providing a detailed job description. Since most of the friction occurs around the beginning and end of the day, when you may have to be earlier or later than usual, it is well worth sorting out arrangements that you are both happy with before the difficulty arises, since it is often a feeling of uncertainty, or being taken for granted that causes the problem in childcare arrangements. The most satisfactory arrangement is to agree to pay your childminder or nanny an additional amount per hour when you leave your child longer than the normal time and an agreed procedure about how you will inform her of your plans.

It is worth finding out if your childminder has links with other childminders or any local childminding organisations, since they usually have plans made to help each other out in times of crisis. If your child attends nursery or an out-of-school scheme or your child carer cannot work after a certain time, you need to have at least two willing people who would be prepared to collect and mind your child until you can pick him up. You also need to have a list of several obliging 'helpers' if you collect children from school. Don't just rely on one person, in case she/he is unable to help for any reason. Many working mothers neglect to go to these lengths, thinking that the occasions when things go wrong are few and far between and they will cope somehow. They may be right. However, to avoid unnecessary stress and anxiety when you find yourself delayed for any reason, it is important to have back-up arrangements. The lack of contingency plans for the one-off emergency can also lead to imagined worry about *'what if ...'* which would be less easily activated with careful planning.

Is your workload the real problem?

Part of the problem for you may lie in coping with guilty feelings about leaving your child, and you may find it is difficult to rid yourself of this form of self-induced stress, even when she is thriving and doing well. Your feelings of anxiety may transfer to the work situation and lead you to lose confidence in yourself and your ability. You may find you get a distorted view of your workload, as tasks which you haven't completed mount up and you find it harder to make decisions. Many working mothers feel overwhelmed by work and work-related issues, but often their real concern is a worry about their child. It is important to recognise whether stress about your work is really rooted elsewhere.

Learn to switch roles

How effective are you at switching roles from work to home?

If you find your mind is full of work problems and you are neglecting relationships at home, you need to practise ways of maintaining the two separate identities more rigidly. Below are some ideas to help you.

♦ Have a focal point travelling from work when you make a conscious act of switching your thoughts from one role to the next. For example, when I reach the garage, five minutes from the childminder's, I will put all thoughts of work out of my head and think about the evening with my children.

♦ Play a tape of music and sing along or listen to the radio to provide a 'break', when you are able to switch off and leave problems and thoughts related to work behind you.

♦ Learn to be disciplined and say to yourself, 'I will not think about this now' when worries about work enter your head while you are at home.

♦ If it helps, change your work clothes when you get home and consciously put on a 'new identity'.

♦ Find ways of distracting your mind from work-related thoughts at home by involving yourself in activities that demand your full attention and that you particularly enjoy, such as playing games with the children, planning where to go on holiday, doing crosswords, making up stories for the children at bedtime.

♦ Set aside a time each evening for yourself and plan to have a treat ready, however small. Make a list of the things you enjoy and which help you to relax, e.g. have a relaxing bath planned with your favourite oils in which to immerse yourself when the children are in bed, rent a favourite video, buy yourself a different magazine, book a beautician who works evenings to give you a massage or facial. Many working mothers feel treating themselves in this way is far too indulgent, but you will find even the smallest treat helps you to feel better and relegate problems from work to the back of your mind for a while.

Now that you have reached the end of this section, you may be feeling more confident about yourself and more aware of ways to help you maintain a satisfactory balance between your work, your family life and your personal wants and needs. The next section concentrates more closely on how you can improve your relationships with your children and considers other child-related issues which may be of concern to you.

You and Your Child

This section is concerned with helping you to enhance the relationship you have with your children, whether they are toddlers or teenagers.

A lot of time, energy and emotion is spent in the task of mothering; it is a complex and demanding experience for which most of us have had little training, planning or preparation. The relationship you develop with your children has the capacity to affect all the other parts of your life. It can have a profound effect on your work, your self-esteem and your relationships with other people, and may significantly influence your hopes and expectations for the future; it can have you sobbing into the nappies or overwhelmed with pride and happiness.

This section helps you to reflect on the ways in which you interact with your child or children, and the relationship you are developing with them. Exercises, questionnaires, case studies and sample conversations help you to think about ways of encouraging your child to become more communicative, cooperative and independent.

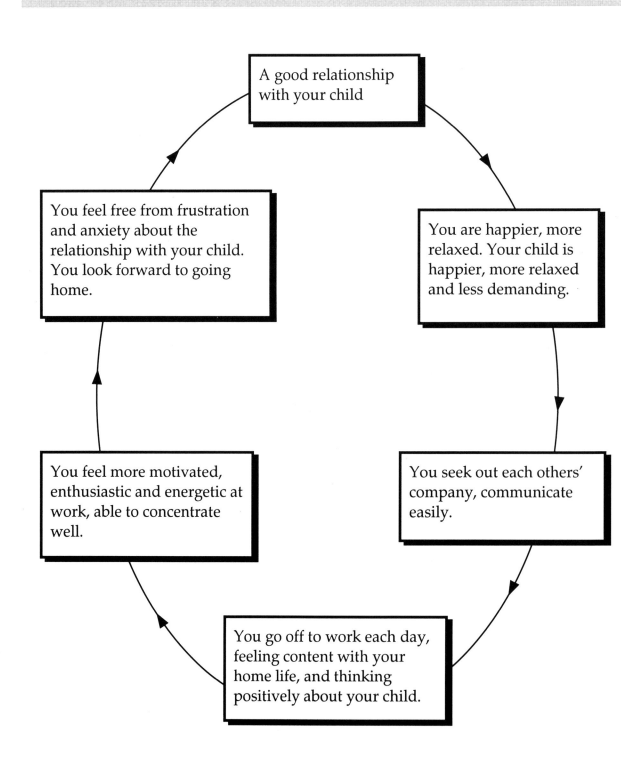

A good relationship with your child

You are happier, more relaxed. Your child is happier, more relaxed and less demanding.

You seek out each others' company, communicate easily.

You go off to work each day, feeling content with your home life, and thinking positively about your child.

You feel more motivated, enthusiastic and energetic at work, able to concentrate well.

You feel free from frustration and anxiety about the relationship with your child. You look forward to going home.

A poor relationship with your child may negatively influence your ability to cope at work

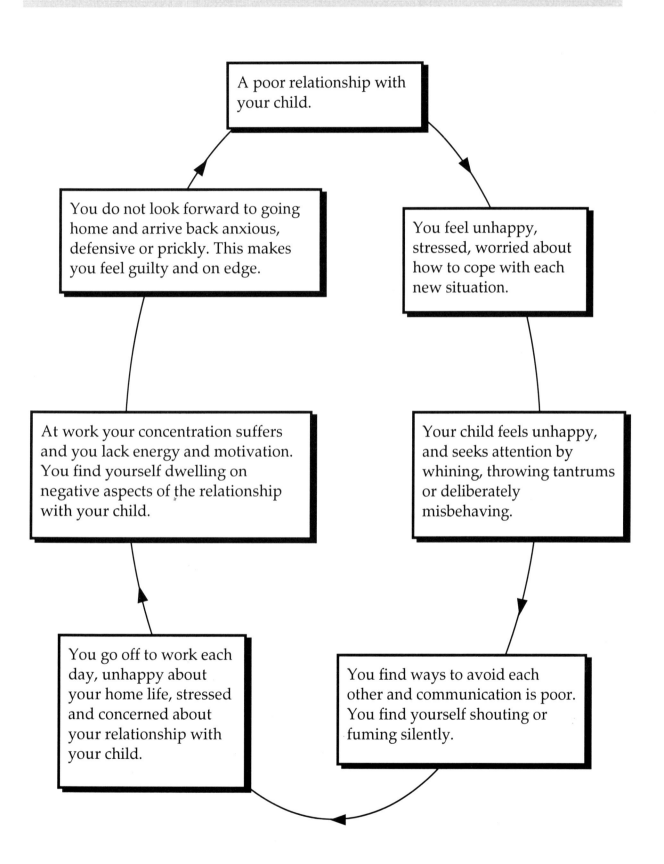

A poor relationship with your child.

You feel unhappy, stressed, worried about how to cope with each new situation.

Your child feels unhappy, and seeks attention by whining, throwing tantrums or deliberately misbehaving.

You find ways to avoid each other and communication is poor. You find yourself shouting or fuming silently.

You go off to work each day, unhappy about your home life, stressed and concerned about your relationship with your child.

At work your concentration suffers and you lack energy and motivation. You find yourself dwelling on negative aspects of the relationship with your child.

You do not look forward to going home and arrive back anxious, defensive or prickly. This makes you feel guilty and on edge.

Your conflicting roles as a working mother

All of us want a warm, loving relationship with our children, and when things don't turn out the way we had hoped we are quick to put the blame onto ourselves and our role as *working* mothers. We torture ourselves unmercifully with images of ourselves as better mothers. Even if things are going well, we carry a haunting feeling that relationships with our children would be even better if we were *not* working.

My child wouldn't behave like this if I were at home all the time.

If only I'd been home to entertain his school friends he'd have a better social life.

If only I could have been there when she hurt her leg things would have been different.

If only I had time to cook balanced meals, I'd feel ......

I used to do lots of things with my mother – if only I had time to share interesting activities with my child.

If only I could be at every parents' meeting, the teachers would know me and things would be better.

If only I could be there when the children get home from school they would feel more secure.

There isn't enough time for me to spend with my child so the relationship is bound to suffer.

I wouldn't feel the need to buy him so much if I spent more time with him.

Things mothers say: have you ever made any similar comments?

Instead of thinking in a negative way and blaming your dual role for problems within the relationship, examine the interactions you have with your children and work out how things could be different. By discovering ways in which you, as a working mother, can build more positive and effective relationships with your children, you will ensure that life at work and at home is as rewarding and sustaining as possible for the benefit of everyone.

Understanding your relationship with your child

The more clearly you understand what kind of mother you want to be, and the more certain you are about the type of relationship you want to build with your son or daughter, the clearer your choices and the directions you want to follow become.

Remembering how you felt about your parents will help you to understand better your own relationship with your child. The behaviours, attitudes and language you use as a parent are often a result of the way you were brought up yourself. Even if you disagreed with some of the ways your parents treated you, you may behave in similar ways towards your own children because it has become familiar.

It is worth doing some serious self-reflection to see if you can discover how far, and in what ways, your own upbringing influences your current behaviour (see next page).

If you don't work hard you'll end up on the scrap heap.

I wish I'd had your chances.

You are a bully.

Boys don't cry / Girls don't climb trees.

You are so ungrateful.

This is hurting me more than it is hurting you.

You do as I say or else...

Let me do that for you / I know what's best.

You can't be too careful.

How many times have I told you to...

You decided to do it – now reap the consequences.

It's good to see you / to have you around.

I love you.

You always cheer me up.

You will do well.

I can count on you.

You are a great artist / cook / writer / tennis player.

You are great.

I'm proud of what you did.

Do as you think best.

You can do it.

Thank you for being so thoughtful / kind / reliable.

Did your parents behave in any of these negative ways?

Criticising you for a small part of a task without noticing the rest had been tackled well ☐

Standing over you while you were doing a task ☐

Fussing over illness/ignoring illness ☐

Punishing you unnecessarily ☐

Giving in to you too much ☐

Getting into frightening rages ☐

Analysing everything ☐

Calling you names, being sarcastic ☐

Always knowing everything ☐

Being insensitive to your needs and feelings ☐

Setting too high goals for you ☐

Withholding positive feedback and treats ☐

Taking over your work, friends and life ☐

Venting anger against you which they felt against themselves or others ☐

Encouraging you to go for the easy options ☐

Did your parents behave in any of these positive ways?

Treating you with respect at all times ☐

Asking for your opinion on family issues ☐

Negotiating over rules ☐

Being sensitive to your needs and feelings ☐

Encouraging you to make your own decisions ☐

Accepting you despite your faults ☐

Celebrating your strengths ☐

Encouraging you to make your own decisions ☐

Allowing you to make mistakes ☐

Showing a constructive interest in your work and friends ☐

Showing you physical affection ☐

Allowing you to find your own solutions to problems ☐

Is your history repeating itself with your own children?

In your interactions with your children have you ever found yourself saying or doing things that you hated your parents saying or doing to you? Even with the best will in the world you may find your words and actions spilling out automatically, especially when you are stressed and anxious. Do you find yourself nurturing, or striving to nurture, your children in the same way as you were nurtured? Even if you feel positive about the way your parents interacted with you, consider whether or not it is an effective way to build positive relationships with your own child. Your parents' beliefs may be out of date in today's culture or inappropriate for you as a working mother.

There are two exercises to complete on the following pages.

The first exercise will help you to reflect on your own upbringing and to become more aware of how your own experiences may have influenced the way you interact with your child. The second exercise helps you to think about the mother you hope to be.

Experiences from my own family Complete the following statements as you remember them now.

One thing I liked about how my parents treated me:

Mother	
Father	

One thing I did not like about how my parents treated me:

Mother	
Father	

My parents disciplined me by:

Mother

Father

My parents encouraged me by:

Mother

Father

My parents discouraged me by:

Mother

Father

My parents praised me for:

Mother

Father

My parents spent time with me doing:

Mother

Father

The thing I liked best about being a child in my family was:

The thing I liked least about being a child in my family was:

Some of the things I would have changed are:

What I would ideally like my child to think and say about me

Complete the sentences that follow as you would *like* your child to do.

My mother shows she loves me by ...

My mother rewards me by ...

My mother disciplines me by ...

The nicest thing I do with my mother is ...

My relationship with my mother is ...

The thing I like best about my mother is ...

My mother shows she understands me by ...

My mother helps me be independent by ...

When my mother and I argue she ...

How cooperative is your child?

Fill in the following questionnaires to find out which aspects of the relationship with your child are causing you most concern and putting a strain on your personal and professional life. Mark the appropriate response.

	Yes	Sometimes	No
1. If I ask my child to do something by a certain time, I can rely on its being done.	☐	☐	☐
2. Against my better judgement, I give in to my child's requests because I haven't the energy to argue.	☐	☐	☐
3. When I see my child's teacher/playgroup leader/friend's mother, it would not surprise me to hear about how cooperative and pleasant he has been.	☐	☐	☐
4. I can ask my child three or four times to do something and even then she may not obey.	☐	☐	☐
5. I feel pleased with the way I deal with uncooperative children.	☐	☐	☐

	Yes	Sometimes	No
6. There are certain times when I dread being with my child (e.g. in the car, in supermarkets, with relations).	☐	☐	☐
7. My child volunteers to help me.	☐	☐	☐
8. I find myself doing jobs that I could give to the children because it is less hassle.	☐	☐	☐
9. I can rely on my children to behave well with visitors, in public places etc.	☐	☐	☐
10. I have struggles with my child about the same things every day (e.g. getting up, washing, chores, homework, eating).	☐	☐	☐
11. My child will cooperate with my requests when I am not there to supervise.	☐	☐	☐

Questions on cooperation

Scores for Questions 1, 3, 5, 7, 9 and 11

Q1	3	5	7	9	11

= ☐

If you have marked yes score 3, sometimes 1 and no 0.

Scores for Questions 2, 4, 6, 8 and 10

Q2	4	6	8	10

= ☐

If you have marked yes score 0, sometimes 1 and no 3.

Total score ☐

Scores between 24 and 33

Few problems over cooperation. Your child is behaving in a cooperative way and it is unlikely that you have a major problem in this area. You have a firm foundation on which to make any changes. Check that fear and punishment are not your child's main motivators for cooperating.

Scores between 8 and 24

Some problems over cooperation. You have a cooperative child on many occasions but her behaviour can cause you problems when you are least expecting it. This may leave you feeling drained because you cannot rely on her cooperation when you need it most. You may find yourself veering from punishment to praise as you try to find what works best.

Scores below 8

Some real difficulties over cooperation. You are finding your child difficult to deal with on frequent occasions and often feel unable to cope with the demands she makes on your time, energy and patience. You sometimes feel that your strategies for dealing with her need a major rethink. Your work may suffer as your mind tends to stray to concerns at home.

How independent is your child?

	True	False
1. I am more protective of my child than most mothers I know.	☐	☐
2. I don't intervene automatically when my child is having difficulty with fixing something or working something out.	☐	☐
3. I think there are very few choices my child is capable of making without me.	☐	☐
4. If my child forgot something for which he would be in trouble, I would not make myself late for work in order to get it to him.	☐	☐
5. Even though I had planned an evening out, I would stay in if my children did not want to be left.	☐	☐
6. I am willing to consider that what looks like a bad choice to me, may be a good choice for my child.	☐	☐
7. Friends tell me I do too much for my child.	☐	☐
8. I make sure I allow time each week for my own interests and hobbies.	☐	☐
9. I believe my child's behaviour reflects on my competence as a mother.	☐	☐

	True	False
10. I do not do many things for my child that she could do for herself.	☐	☐
11. I find myself getting angry with anyone who criticises my child.	☐	☐
12. People tell me my child is independent for her age.	☐	☐

Questions on independence and self-reliance

Scores for Questions 1, 3, 5, 7, 9 and 11

Q1	3	5	7	9	11

= ☐

If you have marked False, score 3; for True, score 0.

Scores for Questions 2, 4, 6, 8, 10 and 12

Q2	4	6	8	10	12

= ☐

If you have marked True, score 3; for False, score 0.

Total score ☐

Scores between 24 and 36

You go out of your way to encourage your child's independence as you have recognised the importance of letting him learn from the consequences of his choices. You see the importance of meeting your own needs as well as his. Check that he doesn't feel pressured with too much responsibility.

Scores between 9 and 24

You have some problems in letting go and may worry unnecessarily about your child's ability to cope on his own. Sometimes you feel guilty if you put your own interests first. At other times you feel happy to let him make his own choices and trust him to get on by himself and find he copes well.

Scores under 9

You seem to be doing too much for your child and may later wonder why he feels held back, becomes too clinging, or shows disrespect rather than gratitude. You seem to put your own interests last on most occasions. You may find difficulty in seeing your child as an independent person, which results in your seeing his actions as directly reflecting your competence as a mother. You may feel that other children of the same age are given too much freedom and lack discipline.

How well do you communicate with your child?

	True	Occasionally	False
1. My child says I don't listen to her.	☐	☐	☐
2. My child confides in me about important things, e.g. fears, bullying, relationships.	☐	☐	☐
3. My child finds my weak spots and often hurts me with comments she makes.	☐	☐	☐
4. I avoid giving advice when my child asks me what he should do about work, friends, money etc.	☐	☐	☐
5. I find myself labelling my child as difficult, clever, quiet, hyperactive etc., and talking and thinking about her in this way.	☐	☐	☐
6. I make sure I find time to chat to my child every day and listen attentively to her news which she enjoys telling me.	☐	☐	☐
7. Much of my conversation with my child seems to consist of instructions, and dos and don'ts.	☐	☐	☐
8. I am physically demonstrative with my child to show I love and care for her.	☐	☐	☐
9. Although conversations seem to start off well, I find my child seems to take what I say the wrong way and the conversation is over before it's begun.	☐	☐	☐
10. There are only a few occasions I can think of when I regret how I have spoken to my child.	☐	☐	☐
11. I can discuss personal issues with my child without causing him embarrassment, or feeling embarrassed myself.	☐	☐	☐

Questions on communication

Scores for Questions 1, 3, 5, 7, 9 and 11

Q1	3	5	7	9	11		
						=	

If you have marked False score 3, Occasionally score 1, True score 0

Scores for Questions 2, 4, 6, 8, and 10

Q2	4	6	8	10		
					=	

If you have marked True score 3, False score 0.

Total score ____

Scores between 25 and 33

You communicate well with your child and have found a way of helping through listening well yet recognising when she needs to be left alone. There may be things you cannot talk about but you are willing to wait until the time is right. You may have cross words but these are easily forgotten. Keep working on your communication skills.

Scores between 12 and 25

On many days there is no problem for you in talking to your child, and everything appears to be going well for both of you. Then there is a breakdown in communication that comes out of the blue and leaves you feeling puzzled or upset. You may take this to heart and find it difficult to be positive as you do not feel you have put a foot wrong. Check that you are listening rather than giving instructions on these occasions.

Scores under 12

You seem to be having real difficulties in communicating with your child: she may seem so contrary at times, either ignoring you or becoming angry. At times you may find you think of her as difficult or unable to change and do not know what to do for the best. You are hurt by her behaviour and want change.

Your relationship with your child

How to communicate effectively with children, and how to encourage cooperation and independence are three aspects of the mother–child relationship that are a source of concern for many working mothers. We will look at each in turn.

Although many of the working mothers who took part in our survey felt happy with this aspect of their relationship, some of the difficulties that were mentioned included not having enough time to talk to their children, feeling unable to talk about various topics such as relationships, growing up, behaviour, school work, in a way they would have liked. Some mothers described how conversations that seemed to start out fine ended in slanging matches or silence, and how disappointed they were when children wouldn't confide in them or take their advice or preferred watching TV to talking to them. Being physically demonstrative with their child was difficult for some mothers.

What women told us Janet: *'I seem to have to tread so carefully with my daughter – I can't believe she's so sensitive. We've had such rows over trivial matters. I have a rule now to criticise nothing. So if she asks me, for instance, if I like her shoes, even though I think the colour is ghastly, I always make some positive comments like "That style looks really good on you." I can't remember my mother needing to treat me so carefully.'*

Nina: *'I don't know what to do about the children's passion for favourite TV programmes. When I get home I'd like to think they were pleased to see me but I'd cause a major row if I suggested they turn the TV off. I worry about this.'*

Other mothers found TV a help.

Jill: *'They get poor attention/love when I'm very tired after work and I feel guilty that I'm pleased to find them engrossed with their programme and not clamouring for my attention.'*

Anne: *'I wish he would talk about his worries with me. I think he gets bullied but I can't get him to talk about it.'*

Leslie: *'It really makes me scream inside when they say "You don't talk to me – you're too busy all the time."'*

Marilyn worried about the messages she was giving to her daughter when she said: *'I didn't tell you because you were too tired.'*

Jo: *'I often think – I didn't mean to say that – it just came out.'*

Encouraging children to become independent and self-reliant

Many working mothers in our survey felt helping children to take responsibility for themselves was a particularly important though difficult task. As their own life as working mothers needs to be super-organised and efficient, this often results in their taking over the children's lives far too much. In the same way doing too much for children seemed a way of compensating for not being around as much as they would have liked because of work commitments. It was difficult for some mothers to get children to do things for themselves in spite of a real determination to achieve this. Several women described feeling swamped by the concerns of other family members and the day-to-day running of the home, and spent most evenings and weekends dealing with these rather than spending time on their own work, hobbies or other leisure activities.

What women told us
Jane: *'When my child said "I need you Mum" even though she was at school, I wondered what I was doing wrong.'*

Anna: *'I know it would be better to let the kids learn how to do the washing and make them tidy up more, but I honestly can't be bothered – it's easier to do it myself and then I know I don't have to keep thinking, "is it done?".'*

Jenny: *'I have this stupid guilt thing about home-made cakes so I spend time doing this when I could and should be doing something else. I don't even like baking.'*

Marilyn: *'It can really get to me when they say things like "Mandy's mother doesn't make her do her own lunch" or "Why are you always working?".'*

Encouraging the children to cooperate

Questions about discipline and cooperation provoked a lot of response. Some of the difficulties mentioned included: getting children to do what they were told, dealing with temper tantrums, constantly feeling like the enemy issuing orders, getting tired of the wearing battles over bedtimes, schoolwork, clothes, manners, confusion as to the best way to discipline children, feeling on edge, angry and disappointed with the children and with themselves, and giving in because of weariness and then feeling ineffective and depressed.

What women told us
Annie: *'I discipline my children badly by shouting and losing control and then feel incredibly guilty.'*

Cathryn: *'There seem to be more rows about time than anything else – getting out of bed on time, keeping people waiting, meeting me on time ...'*

Rose: *'I think I am far too sensitive and over-react to remarks about my meanness or the rules I set and then things get worse. I can't seem to stay calm.'*

Janet: *'I get mad when I ask the children to do something and am ignored but as soon as their father asks, they do it. I think this annoys me more than their disobedience.'*

Ruth: *'The children seem to be less cooperative when they know it will bother me if they are not. For instance when my mother-in-law is around or when the health visitor calls I have more trouble, and then I'm bad-tempered for the rest of the day.'*

Jo: *'I sometimes do and say things I swore I'd never say to my children.'*

Through reading other mothers' comments and answering the questionnaire, you may have recognised some of the less helpful ways in which you currently relate to your child. The tension, disappointment and guilt resulting from unsatisfactory interactions with your child will considerably detract from your enjoyment of life as a working mother.

Using what you have read to remind you, fill in the questionnaire below.

My main problem in communicating with my child is:

My main problem in helping my child to be more cooperative is:

My main problem in helping my child to be more independent / self-reliant is:

Developing quality relationships

The rest of this section focuses on ways in which you, as a working mother, can build a more effective relationship with your child and thereby gain greater happiness and satisfaction in your life at home and at work.

♦ The first part is concerned with helping you to improve your communication with your child.

♦ The second part is concerned with helping you to encourage cooperation in your child.

♦ The third part is concerned with helping to encourage independence in your child.

Improving your communication with your child

The quality of the relationship with your child depends very much on the quality of your communication with her. Improving your communication skills by listening and responding more effectively, and making it easier for your child to talk and listen to you, will have a dramatic effect on your feelings for each other.

Listening to your child Listening to your child involves not only hearing his words and being sensitive to the feelings behind the words, but also being aware of all the non-verbal signals he might reveal: the frightened eyes, the confident cock of the head, the downcast face, which can say so much more than words.

How can we learn to listen better? The way you respond to your child is the key to convincing him that you care enough to listen. An important first step is to accept your child's feelings. This is easier said than done because many of us have been brought up to believe that feelings of anger, fear, disappointment or anxiety are wrong and should not be expressed. We may find difficulty in responding appropriately to children's outbursts of *'I hate my teacher'* or *'I am so scared of going to the dentist'*, or *'I'm fed up with all my boring toys'* or *'You never play with me'*, and react by denying what they have said.

Imagine this conversation:

Child: *'I really hate Spelling and I'm bad at it.'*

Mother: *'Don't be silly – you've always been one of the best in the class.'*

Child: *'But now I'm not, and I don't like it.'*

Mother: *'You are just having an off-day – of course you like it – you'll feel differently tomorrow.'*

If you think about what is happening here, you can see that the conversation is starting to turn into an argument. The more the child's feelings are denied the more he is made to feel confused and cross. The child's mother becomes increasingly irritated with the child, who cannot see what *she* knows to be true. Both end up feeling angry and misunderstood and the relationship suffers.

Imagine something similar happening to you.

You: *'I hate driving in the dark when it's raining – I don't drive at all well.'*

Partner: *'Don't be silly – you are a perfectly good driver in all weathers.'*

You: *'But tonight I felt really on edge in the traffic.'*

Partner: *'You're feeling tired. Have a cup of coffee and forget about it.'*

How would you feel? Annoyed? Misunderstood? Frustrated?

An automatic denial of our feelings can leave us feeling as confused and cross as a child. People who respond in this way often have the best of intentions to help us feel better, but unfortunately their remarks may have completely the opposite effect.

Here are some traditional ways of responding to the child who is voicing her concern about her Maths. Can you identify with any of them?

The over-sympathetic mother

Child: *'I really hate Spelling – I'm bad at it.'*

Mother: *'Oh what a shame – I'm so upset. I'll worry myself silly if we don't get this sorted out.'*

How would you feel if you received this response?

I would feel ...

The amateur psychologist mother

Child: *'I really hate Spelling – I'm bad at it.'*

Mother: *'How long ago did this happen? Was it when you fell out with Josie and stopped sitting next to her for Spelling? Are you feeling left out?'*

How would you feel if you received this response?

> I would feel ...

The 'know-it-all' mother

Child:　'*I really hate Spelling – I'm bad at it.*'

Mother:　'*You know what you should do! Go to school tomorrow and make sure you work twice as hard as usual. Bring the books home and I'll sort out where you are going wrong.*'

How would you feel if you received this response?

> I would feel ...

The critical mother

Child:　'*I really hate Spelling – I'm bad at it.*'

Mother:　'*You've not been paying enough attention. You are a real time-waster. You'll never get on in life if you can't spell you know.*'

How would you feel if you received this response?

> I would feel ...

These are some typical ways in which mothers may talk to children. You have put yourself in the child's shoes and made a guess as to how you would feel. It may have helped you to recognise that if you are upset, hurting or confused you want understanding, not pity, false reassurance, a mini-analysis, or worst of all, someone telling you that you shouldn't feel that way!

What you want is someone to listen attentively and non-judgementally to your concerns. You need to feel sufficiently comfortable in the relationship before you can begin to explore your feelings of hurt, anger, disappointment or worry. If you are offered this quality of listening then you may come to understand and cope with such feelings yourself. This is also the quality of listening that children want and need. They, too, can understand and cope better with their feelings if they have been listened to sensitively.

Becoming an effective listener

Becoming an effective listener requires your full attention – eye contact, a posture that says, 'I'm listening', and a way of responding that enables the child to feel understood. It means allowing children to express how they feel and what they think, without fear of rejection. It does not mean that you agree or disagree with what they are saying, rather that you show a willingness to accept that they feel as they do. If you want children to feel you are really listening, then you need to be able to 'get into their shoes' and 'see the world through their eyes' and communicate this understanding back to them. It takes considerable thought and a lot of effort to listen well and it is worth taking time to learn and practise some of the following techniques, which have been found particularly effective.

Using reflective listening

Reflective listening involves recognising what the child feels and means and then *stating* this meaning so that she feels understood and accepted.

Example

Daughter: *'I'm fed up with Annie – she never meets me at the time we've agreed.'*

Mother: *'Sounds as if you are really annoyed with her always being late.'*

This response shows acceptance and concern, recognises what she is feeling, and encourages her to continue the conversation.

A more likely response might have been:

Daughter: *'I'm fed up with Annie – she never meets me at the time we've agreed.'*

Mother: *'Why don't you arrive late for her next time and see how she feels!'*

   or

   'Some people are always late, they'll never change'

   or

   'Are you sure you really agreed on the time – you know how forgetful you are sometimes!'

111

These responses do not accept the daughter's feelings and may leave her feeling even more angry with her friend, at the same time feeling misunderstood and let down by her mother. She is unlikely to continue the conversation amicably and may well start to argue with her mother, defending her friend or herself from further attack. Either way, the relationship has not been enhanced by this conversation.

More important than our words, is our attitude towards our child. If we respond without demonstrating interest, concern or compassion in our actions, facial expression, tone of voice, then whatever we say will be seen as putting on an act.

If we can demonstrate by our body language that we are listening attentively and have a caring attitude, even a few words in response may be all that are needed.

Son:	*'Mum, I think I'll stop going to Youth Club.'*
Mother:	*'Really?'*
Son:	*'It's boring now that John and Andrew have left.'*
Mother:	*'Is it?'*
Son:	*'It would be more fun if I could persuade some of the other boys in my class to go.'*
Mother:	*'I see.'*
Son:	*'That's what I think I'll do. I'll ask John tomorrow if he is interested.'*

You can see that this kind of response encourages a child to come up with his own answers. He is using you as a sounding board to think things through.

A more usual type of response might have been.

Son:	*'Mum, I think I'll stop going to Youth Club.'*
Mother:	*'Oh I wouldn't do that if I were you. You've only just joined.'*
Son:	*'It's boring now that John and Andrew have left.'*
Mother:	*'Can't you do anything without having those two around? They don't seem to be your type to me.'*
Son:	*'What do you mean not my type? You are always criticising my friends.'* (Son stalks off – end of conversation.)

You may be thinking children would be irritated if you responded reflectively but this is seldom the case unless, of course, you merely repeat their words exactly. Often they have not verbalised their feelings before. Having their feelings acknowledged and described in a way that shows you understand, gives children real comfort and helps them to understand themselves better.

Constructing a reflective response

1. Identify what your child is feeling.

2. Try to think of a word that sums up the emotion. You can use the same word the child has used but it demonstrates real understanding if you can capture her feelings with an accurate alternative.

3. Put the word into a sentence that reflects the feeling and the content of the statement

Try the next exercise.

Here are five statements a child might make to her mother. For each statement write down a word or two to describe what the child might be feeling, and a response you would make to show the child you understand the feeling.

Child's statement	Her feeling	Your response
Example: *'I'll be glad when this is all over, it's going on and on'*	Bored	*'You seem really fed up with it.'*
'I don't know whether to go on the outing or not.'		
'I can't seem to make her understand no matter what I say.'		
'I was the only one not asked to Martin's party.'		
'Everyone laughed when I couldn't work the computer.'		

It is sometimes difficult to find immediate answers even though you are concentrating on the task, but with practice this type of responding becomes more natural and easier.

Some responses might be:

♦ Sounds like you are finding it difficult to make up your mind.

♦ You seem frustrated in trying to get her to grasp what you mean.

♦ You sound disappointed to have been left off the invitation.

♦ Sounds like that was embarrassing for you.

In the real situation, you have to think quickly and it may be more difficult to come up with the right word. *It doesn't matter if you don't get it exactly right.*

No one can be sure what another person is feeling or thinking, so use reflective statements tentatively.

Example:

You seem to be ...

Am I right in thinking ...?

You sound as if ...

These phrases strike the right note. If you are wrong your child will soon let you know.

Example:

Mother: *'You sound disappointed that Anne can't come to the party.'*

Daughter: *'No, I'm glad – I want to play outside and she doesn't like to.'*

The important point is that you made the effort to listen and understand and this is what is appreciated by the child.

Using reflective listening may not work right away. When children are familiar with a different style of communication, your first attempts at responding in this way may meet with a blank expression, embarrassment, or plain astonishment. Don't give up. Be patient and give your child a chance to adjust to your new style of responding.

Don't overdo reflective listening; use your discretion as to the appropriate response. Many conversations with children consist of casual remarks and if your child said, for example, *'Mum, it's hot in here'*, to which you replied *'So you're finding it really warm'*, your child would begin to think you had gone loopy! Be sensitive to the occasion. Its use is most appropriate when dealing with children's negative feelings. When we are tempted to 'jolly along' the upset child, to deny a child's angry feelings, to moralise when a child is being thoughtless or mean, by changing our response to a reflective remark we can encourage real communication.

Questions we have been asked by women in our groups

What's wrong with saying, I know how you feel?

This phrase is somehow never very comforting and for many of us it's like a red rag to a bull. The child who receives this response is no doubt thinking, as we may do, *'No you don't. How can you know how I feel? You aren't me and haven't a clue what I'm going through.'* Telling someone you know how they feel doesn't take much effort. It is a phrase that is used by many as an automatic response to any expression of another's feelings. When you take the trouble to reflect the child's feelings carefully, he knows you understand and want to see things from his perspective.

Won't children think everything they say and feel is OK if we use reflective listening?

There is a great deal of difference between agreeing with how children feel and acknowledging how they feel. If we agree with the feelings we prevent them from exploring concerns for themselves.

Example:

Son: *'I'm really mad with John. He said some horrible things about me in front of the others. He didn't care how I felt.'*

Mother: *'He is mean. That's an awful thing to do. He obviously doesn't think much of you – you're better off without him as a friend.'*

It is very likely the conversation would end here. It could have gone something like this:

Son: *'I'm really mad with John. He said some horrible things about me in front of the others. He didn't care how I felt.'*

Mother: *'That must have been hard to take.'*

Son: *'Yes it was, and I know he was only trying to pay me back for what I did to him last week.'*

(The temptation here is to ask *'What did you do to him last week?'* but this would not be useful as it would divert the conversation away from the discussion of feelings and may feel intrusive to the son.)

Mother: *'You think it was his way of getting his own back?'*

Son: *'Yes it was, but it was really mean and he made me feel upset.'*

Mother: *'You know it was for revenge, but you are still hurt.'*

Son: *'Yes I am. I'm going to ring him up and tell him.'*

In this conversation, the mother has accepted her son's feelings, helped him think constructively about his experience, to clarify how he felt, and thereby helped him decide what to do about the situation with his friend.

There are some remarks children make that we may find difficult to listen to.

Examples:

'I hate Billy (baby brother) – *he's noisy and smelly.'*

'I hate Grandma (in her presence) – *she's always bossing me about.'*

'I hate you!'

To the first example we usually reply with a gentle rebuke such as *'Oh no you don't, you love him really. Give him a cuddle and say you're sorry.'* It would be much better to respond reflectively: *'You sound very cross with him – babies can be a nuisance when they cry so much'*; (you are saying in effect, *'I understand you are feeling angry with him and I accept that you feel that way'*). It is then appropriate to give the child an outlet for his anger or jealousy. *'I usually put some music on when he makes me cross – do you want to do that?'*

The second and third examples usually bring out the worst in us! We are likely to send the child to her room, shout in anger, take her silently out of the room holding her *very firmly* by the arm so that she gets the message! All these reactions will leave us feeling drained and furious. We feel mad with the child and embarrassed in front of our own mother who may add fuel to the fire with her own well-chosen remarks. A reflective response in this situation takes considerable courage but will often take the heat and embarrassment out of the situation. *'You seem very cross with grandma for telling you what to do.'* You can then go on to say, *'I don't like the words you used or the way you said it. We'll talk about this later when you can find another way of telling me'.*

> *Won't children think I am being rather strange saying their words back to them? Anyway, I think I'd feel rather odd repeating things like this.*

Some children may be surprised when you try reflective listening at first, and wonder where all your questions have gone! They will soon appreciate your new style, however, as it will feel less intrusive to them. Many children won't even notice that you are using reflective listening (unless of course you merely parrot back their words exactly). They *will* be aware of your concern to understand their feelings and the situation as *they* see it. Some parents have said that using reflective listening makes them feel as if they are in a play and you, too, may feel unnatural responding in this way initially. Think of it as a new skill to be learned and practised, which will come to be a natural way of responding in time. Effort and patience will pay off as the relationship with your child improves.

Yes, you will! Reflective listening can be overdone. We are not suggesting reflective listening becomes your only way of responding. Think of it as an important skill to be used when your child needs a sensitive response to her feelings.

Summary of points to remember

♦ Quality communication leads to a quality relationship.

♦ Communication begins by listening effectively.

♦ Listening well involves demonstrating your interest and concern through attentive body language and empathic responses.

♦ Criticising, moralising, pitying, lecturing and threatening antagonise children and lead to poorer relationships.

♦ Reflective listening involves hearing the child's words, the feelings behind the words and rephrasing the statement so the child feels understood. It is not parroting.

Helping children to explore options and make decisions

By listening reflectively to your child, you will help her to feel understood, and to clarify her feelings and needs. It may well be that your supportive help is sufficient in itself to enable her to decide what course of action to take. There are other times, however, when she will need more structured help from you in making decisions. You can help her to explore her options and choose solutions that seem most appropriate for her. Recognise that helping children to choose options is not the same thing as giving advice. If you give children advice each time they ask you what to do in a given situation, they never learn to solve their own problems. They may become overly dependent on you for advice and quick to blame you when things go wrong. Aim to help them learn to make their own decisions by taking them through the decision-making process step by step

1. Use reflective listening to help your child understand and clarify her feelings.

Daughter: *'James is upsetting me, he doesn't talk to me any more.'*
Response: *'Sounds like you are fed up with being ignored.'*

Continue in this way to allow her to voice her concerns.

2. Help her to think of the various options she has in dealing with this situation.

(Be careful not to jump too quickly to this stage as most children need time to think through their feelings and concerns.)

'What could you do?'

Try to get most of the ideas from your child, and if you do suggest anything make a tentative suggestion such as: *'Would writing a letter be worth considering?'* rather than: *'Why don't you write him a letter.'*

3. Help her to choose from the list her preferred course of action by considering each of the various options.

'If you did write a letter what is likely to happen?'
'If you asked his friends, how would he react?'
'What do you think would happen if you phoned him?'

4. Help her to set her own goals.

'What exactly have you decided to do?'
'When are you going to do this?'

5. Help her decide on an action plan.

Communicating that you love and value your child

One of the most obvious ways to show your child that you love him is to spend time with him. The quality of the time you spend with him is far more important than the quantity of your time together. Many working mothers who feel guilty about leaving children, and who worry about the small amount of time they can be with them each day, find this notion helpful and reassuring, up to a point. They may continue to feel guilty believing that if they worked less, their children would receive far more quality time and attention. However, this is not borne out by research studies which show that mothers who don't work, don't spend any more quality time with their children than working mothers.

How can you make more quality time together?

Most busy working mothers have such hectic daily schedules that planning regularly to spend quality time with their children on top of all the things that need to be done seems unrealistically optimistic. However, spending quality time with the children doesn't have to mean large chunks of time. Many opportunities to spend time with your children that you let go, or somehow allow to drop to the bottom of your priority list, would only take a 10-minute slot of your time. Ten minutes is usually a possibility on most people's schedules and well worth it if you are both feeling OK. If either of you is having an off-day, don't attempt to interact in activities that need time and attention from both of you. There is nothing worse than trying to get yourself cheerful and positive in order to spend 'quality time' with your child if you are feeling like a piece of chewed string or your child is going out of his way to be ghastly to you; it won't work. On these occasions try to find time to relax, take care of your own needs and have some quality time for yourself. On better days you can plan to spend quality time with your child playing games, teaching him something new, reading a story, singing songs, going on outings together, playing rough and tumble, taking a walk, playing sport – anything that requires personal involvement from both of you. Quality time is time spent listening, talking, accepting, sharing, feeling and interacting with each other. Some of the mothers in our survey had organised their day to make sure that they had quality time with their child.

Tina: *'I make sure that getting ready for bed each night is a special time. I always play with him in the bath and tell him a story about my day and the people at work which I can usually make quite funny. I do invent characters from time to time! We have a cuddle and a book story and then he plays with my husband and me for a while before he goes to bed.'*

Jo: *'I spend time with my daughter in the late evening when I know a lot of her friends would be in bed, but unless I keep her up late, I don't see her. I ask the babyminder to make sure she gets a sleep in the day.'*

If possible, involve your child in choosing the activities, and the time. If you have more than one child try to make some quality time with each child alone. This may mean thinking of ways in which you could involve your child in some of the jobs you have to do, such as cooking, gardening or shopping. Many children hate shopping but it becomes a fun time if you have your own list of things to find or choose in the supermarket, and there is a meal in a Macdonald's with Mum, on your own, at the end of it. Many of the most memorable quality times don't cost anything. The hour you spent tobogganing, or the time you both got the giggles trying to erect the tent on the lawn, may have been more important for your relationship with each other than an expensive weekend away. Children have excellent memories for these special times with you and will often use them as comforters when they are feeling unhappy or unloved.

If your relationship with your child is not as positive as you would like it to be, and you make a decision to spend more quality time with her, don't expect the situation to improve overnight. There may be a lot of resistance to the idea and some suspicion as to your motives at first. Have patience. Your intention is to convince your child that you want to be with her and that she is valuable, important and loved, so it is crucial to persist.

Communicate your feelings verbally and physically

Some children feel unloved, if that love has not been expressed, even though there is no reason for them to feel this way. We must tell children that we love them over and over again until they are in no doubt at all of our feelings for them. You might find it difficult to actually say the words – some people do – but do make sure you say them. Don't be put off if your child doesn't seem able to accept your words and looks embarrassed: he may need time to get used to hearing you tell him how you feel.

You may want to write a note to let him know you care. If he has been unhappy about school, put a note in his lunchbox: *'Hope you're having a better day today. Love you, Mum'*, or a note on the kitchen table when he gets home: *'Looking forward to seeing you at 6pm. Love you, Mum'*. You may feel it is unnecessary to tell your child you love him as your caring gestures make your love obvious. Yet the concrete expressions of your love and acceptance are also vital in helping him to feel loveable and valuable.

You can also communicate your love by small positive gestures of affection, buying his favourite biscuits, buying a small inexpensive fun item to surprise him, sharing your belongings with him, allowing him extra time to stay up in the evening and watch a show with you. Share yourself with him. Tell him about your childhood, your work, your friends, what you have been reading and what you like to do. Children love to hear personal stories and it helps them to know and understand you better and feel closer to you.

In the same way, children feel truly loved if you communicate your feelings through hugs, kisses, holding hands, or other physical demonstrations of your affection. It goes without saying that you must respect children's feelings about physical closeness, but many children will say *'Oh stop it Mum'* or shrug off the hug out of embarrassment yet deeply appreciate the physical demonstration of your love. It is difficult to judge but most of the time it is better not to err on the side of caution.

Encouraging children to be cooperative

Dealing with an uncooperative child is arguably the most energy and time-sapping, trying, tiring and esteem-lowering struggle that working mothers experience in the course of their hectic day. The daily battle to get children to behave in ways that are acceptable to us and to society can be more difficult for some working mothers than writing a complicated report, or sorting out a major row among office colleagues. To come home at the end of a busy day at work to a toddler who refuses to do what you ask, or a teenager who is behaving like someone demented, can easily make you question how you cope at all.

Cooperation is a cornerstone of an effective relationship and is vital if you are to live more harmoniously. How do we achieve this happy state of affairs?

Taking stock   The first step in changing things for the better for you and your child (or children) is to take stock of the current situation and identify the issues that are causing most difficulty. What is happening on a daily basis? How many and what type of demands are you making on your child? Be honest and write down all the things that you have battles about on a typical day. Remember to include everything since everything you write down represents your time and your energy and is potentially damaging to the relationship.

Read the following examples and then add examples of your own in the spaces provided.

On a typical day, I get into conflict situations with my child about the following:

Morning	Evening
Examples	
My daughter getting up on time	My son leaving toys in a mess
My son refusing breakfast	My daughter arguing about bedtime

Morning	Evening

Mark the issues that are causing you the most difficulty. Are you insisting on too many dos and don'ts? Are you seeing any pattern in the conflict situations? Is the morning the most problematic time? Is one of your children less cooperative than another?

You may recognise that some of your methods for engaging cooperation only work intermittently or do not work at all. You may be unhappy with what is happening and know your relationship with your child is suffering as a result. Nevertheless, it is likely that you will persist with the same ways of doing things because they are familiar, you haven't the energy or knowledge to try anything different or you think new methods may make things worse.

Change is difficult but your motivation for change depends on:

♦ understanding the effect of your current methods on you and your child
♦ desire to change
♦ knowledge of new methods
♦ conviction that new methods are worth trying

Consider some of the methods most commonly used to get children to cooperate. Maybe some of these things were said to you as a child by people in charge of you. Think back to how you felt at the time and mark any words that describe how you felt, or add your own comment in the spaces. If you didn't experience these comments, try to imagine how a child might feel if these methods were used.

'If I hear that word again you'll be sorry!
'If you don't get a move on you'll get a smack!'

These comments would make me feel:

Frightened
Rebellious
Resentful
Other

Making comparisons with other children

'John is never late for his mother – why can't you be like him?'
'I love the way Abby dresses – I wish you didn't always wear black.'

These comments would make me feel:

Worthless
Unlovable
Unable to please
A failure
Other

Labelling and using put-downs

'Do you call this washing-up finished? You are so sloppy – I might as well do it myself.'
'Stop eating your soup like that. Your table manners are disgusting!'

These comments would make me feel:

Helpless
Unappreciated
Misunderstood
Other

Making children feel guilty

'Stop arguing you two – you know you'll bring on my migraine.'
'If you did as you were told, Dad and I wouldn't row so much – your bad behaviour causes all our problems.'

These comments would make me feel:

Worried
Full of remorse
Miserable
Resentful
Other

Ordering children about

'Get up here and sort this room out now!'
'Don't just stand there looking at it – do it!'
'Get off the phone! Move!'

These comments would make me feel:

Frightened
Bullied
Deep resentment
Wanting to get my own back
Other

Blaming and accusing children

'You've left the freezer door open again. Can't you remember to do the simplest thing?'
'All the milk's gone. Do you never think of anyone but yourself?'

These comments would make me feel:

Unlovable
Picked on
Useless
Powerless
Other

Moralising and lecturing to children

'What did you think you'd gain by being rude to Grandma? Don't you know you should always be polite to older people no matter how much you disagree with them. How would you like it if someone spoke like that to you? Make sure you consider the effect on other people before you speak in future.'

These comments would make me feel:

Inferior
Bored
Other

'There's no chance of you getting a good job. You never worked at school and now you're paying the price. I can see you forever on the dole.'
'If you're like this now I dread to think what you'll be like at 15.'
'If you go around with that superior attitude you'll never have a boyfriend. You'll end up without anybody like your Aunty Sally.'

These comments would make me feel:

Doomed
Demotivated
A failure
Other

If you experienced similar feelings to the ones listed when you completed the exercise, you will appreciate the powerful effect such comments may have on children. Although the comments were intended to make children *more* cooperative, and indeed may initially appear to have worked – the child falls silent, does as he is told – the long-term effect of using such methods is likely to be a far more resentful and *less* cooperative child, a child with a wounded inner spirit and low self-esteem.

In the examples we have discussed above, there was a climate of power where the mother's needs took precedence over the child's. In fact, in some power-oriented relationships, the mother may not even think about the child's needs at all. In some families where cooperation is negligible, there is a climate of permissiveness in which mothers fulfil their child's needs at the expense of their own. Here mothers may feel unappreciated, used as doormats, and grow increasingly angry about their child's behaviour. Both power and permissive climates create 'win-lose' situations neither of which allows child or mother to get all or part of what they want.

There *are* alternative methods to encourage children's internally motivated cooperation that are far more acceptable and less emotionally draining for mothers and that have huge benefits for children's self-esteem and confidence. Although we are suggesting strategies for you to use that will encourage your children to cooperate, the methods are more likely to be successful if you are able to create a climate of respect in the family. By this we mean a climate that takes into consideration both your needs and your child's, an emotional climate that encourages children to cooperate because they care about themselves and care about you; a win-win situation that allows everyone involved to get their needs met.

The following are *first-stage skills* that are useful in managing the daily interactions which, with insensitive handling, often escalate into confrontation and misbehaviour.

Make descriptive statements instead of issuing orders, making accusations or demands

The pressure on working mothers that comes from having to manage a huge variety of family and work issues, particularly tight time schedules, often results in a low tolerance of children's misbehaviour. The children's forgetfulness, untidiness or laziness can be the last straw on a particularly difficult day. The way in which you respond to the behaviour, however, is crucial. A thoughtless comment or throwaway remark can create far more difficulty than it is possible to imagine, and can involve you in hours of further hassle and power struggles.

To prevent arguments and keep the focus on *what needs to be done* or *what you want to happen,* refrain from personal remarks that accuse, blame or force compliance. Instead:

Use a firm, clear voice. Do not shout.

Example: Early morning – room left in a mess.

✗ Labelling, complaining
'You are so untidy. How many times do I have to tell you to clear up before we leave in the morning. I'm sick and tired of talking to children who take no notice.'

✓ Make a statement
'Your pyjamas and towel are on the floor.'

Example: Breakfast time.

✗ Sarcasm, labelling
'You've spilled the milk again – that's great! No cereal for the rest of us. You are such a clumsy boy.'

✓ Make a statement
'The milk's spilled – we need a cloth.

When children are criticised, nagged and ordered about, they become roused, resentful, guilty or worried and the problem (tidying up the towels or knocking over the milk) becomes of secondary consideration. You are very likely to get into a heated exchange that you haven't the time or patience to deal with. Describing the problem lets the child focus on what needs to be done.

Result: fewer arguments, the child knows exactly what is of concern to you and is allowed to put things right without interference – end of the interaction (if it does continue you need to use other methods – see Stage 2 and 3 skills).

Use a few words rather than a monologue or a lecture

Examples:

✗ Monologue, lecture

'Anne you've had that saxophone for three months now and I've hardly heard you play it. You promised to practise every day if we bought it for you. It cost us money we can't really afford. You don't keep promises that don't suit you do you?'

✓ Use a few words

'Anne, your saxophone practice.'

✗ Lecture, label

'You're forgetting your trainers again! There they are still sitting in the hall. You mustn't get in trouble again with that games teacher. You are such a scatterbrain!'

✓ Use a few words

'Alec, your trainers.'

When children are subjected to long harangues, lectures and explanations, they learn to turn off and ignore you or fight their own corner. Their apparent inattention or clever retort only adds fuel to the fire. The shorter the reminder, the more effective it usually is, and the less energy and emotion you will expend.

Give facts rather than subjecting children to an inquisition or a telling-off

When you see dirty clothes strewn across the floor, the cereal packets left open, your family lounging around while you slave away, or your best cheese-knife propping open the hamster's cage, you may react with anger and impatience (naturally enough). It may take a good deal of self-discipline to change your angry response to one of information-giving, but it is one way of ensuring the job is done quickly and with the minimum of resentment.

Example:

✗ Accusation

'Who has left these dirty clothes in the bedroom?'

✓ Give facts

'Dirty clothes should be put in the laundry basket-they make the bedroom smelly.'

Do we *always* need to find out who's the culprit? A considerable amount of our time and energy may be used in trying to find out the details of a particular misdemeanour. It may often lead to family rows as each child swears blind it wasn't her and the cross-examination takes on the profile of an O.J. Simpson trial. A no-blame approach where you concentrate on what is needed to put things right *now and in the future,* means everyone feels OK about the outcome. It is the best way, too, of ensuring there is a desire to co-operate even when you are not around.

✗ Telling off, blaming, moaning
'I just wish once in a while you would get your head out of that magazine and help me in the kitchen.'

✓ Give facts
'The potatoes and carrots need peeling for supper. It would help if you would peel them while I get on with the casserole.'

We sometimes expect children (and adults too) to 'know' when we need help. For some inexplicable reason we remain silent about our needs and expectations. We harbour feelings of resentment as we slave away alone in the kitchen making supper for the rest of the family who are watching TV. Our feelings can splutter out inappropriately, and with far more hostility than we had anticipated, playing havoc with our relationships and ensuring that any help is grudgingly offered. We put paid to any chance of encouraging real cooperation. Children are not mind-readers and they will presume that you are perfectly happy cooking away if you don't say anything to the contrary. Most children would choose to watch TV rather than peel carrots, so if no one asks them, that's great by them! Learning to help other people is like learning anything else – you have to be taught.

We need to make clear and specific requests, long before our resentment sets in. *'I need help with the meal'* is a far less useful request than *'I need you to empty the dishwasher and put the dishes and knives and forks in the cupboards and drawers.'* (If you ask only for the dishwasher to be emptied you may not get the contents put away!)

Describe how you feel

It is important to let children know how you feel. It helps them appreciate that you, too, can feel miserable and angry or have an off day, and need space, understanding and support as much as they do. Explaining your feelings may help them appreciate why you can't help with homework, take them in the car to see their friend or deal patiently with a request for extra pocket money.

It's useful to think in terms of 'I-messages' and 'You-messages'. The 'You-message' is often an attack on the child and focuses on her as a source of the fault. An 'I-message' describes how the child's behaviour makes you feel.

Example:

✗ Blaming, moaning
'Can't you stop pestering me and go and play with your toy?'

✓ Describe how you feel
'It's a good idea to leave me alone just now. I'm feeling cross and it's nothing you have done'.

Sometimes a simple statement of how you are feeling can be very effective in achieving future cooperation.

✗ Labelling
'You are so rude butting into the conversation and making out you know it all.'

✓ Describe how you feel
'I don't like it when I am interrupted.'

Try to identify the source of your anger or irritation before confronting your child about an aspect of her behaviour. On most occasions it is the *consequence* of children's behaviour that causes you the problem rather than the behaviour itself. For instance, if your child borrows your scissors and doesn't put them back in your drawer, you most probably get annoyed *because you can't find them when you want to use them.* You don't necessarily object to her using your scissors.

If one of your children persists in playing loud music when you are filling in your tax return you become irritated *because you can't concentrate on your task.* Loud music in different circumstances is not a problem for you.

When you speak to your child about her misconduct it is important to focus on the consequences the behaviour creates for you, rather than the behaviour itself.

✗ Blaming, accusing
'You are so inconsiderate. You never let me know when you are going to be late. Why can't you ring up – it isn't too much to ask is it?'

✓ Construct an 'I-message' which is clear, concise and focuses on how you feel.
An 'I-message' generally has four parts.

Example:

1 **Describe the behaviour (don't blame)**
   'When you are late without letting me know ...'

2 **State your feeling**
   'I get worried that something's happened to you.'

3 **State the consequence**
   'Because I don't know where you are.'

4 **Ask for the change**
   'I'd appreciate you phoning to let me know in future if you are going to be in after 6pm.'

At times of conflict your display of respect may not have the miraculous effect you hoped for! If the response is a shrug of the shoulders or a rude comment you may feel: 'Why do I bother? She's no more cooperative than if I had bellowed at her.' Don't give up! Using respectful communication and modelling cooperative behaviour(as any other behaviour) has a powerful influence on children's sub-sequent behaviour. More open discussion and greater cooperation at a later date are more likely to follow this type of communication than a hostile confrontation.

Say it with a note

When you feel a new way of engaging cooperation is in order because your usual methods are not working or you are too exhausted to get into verbal discussion, let a note do the talking for you.

Children like receiving notes. Toddlers who can only read a few words are able to make sense of a sketch or drawing or will ask an older brother or sister to read the note for them. It makes the child feel important and the note's message is treated in the same way. If you find you are reminding children a thousand times to ensure things happen, write a note instead.

A note on the kitchen table when the children come home from school.

A note on the television, the door of a room, a bicycle can be a very effective reminder and usually ensures cooperation with little fuss and some amusement.

130

Try to apply some of these strategies to situations on page 122 that cause conflict for you. You may use any of the first stage skills we have discussed, whichever seem the most appropriate depending on the age of the child.

Situation I would like to deal with	First-stage skills I might use
Examples *My daughter always leaves the milk out of the refrigerator after she has used it. She says I'm always going on at her*	*I think I will use a note:* Memo Please put me back each time you use me or I'll go sour
My son forgets his dinner money several times a week.	*I am going to use an 'I-message':* *'Ross, when you forget your dinner money, I feel irritated because I am rung up from school each time to find out what's happened, and it disturbs my work time. I would like you to work out a way of making sure you remember it each day. Could you do that?'*
Try your own examples from page 122	

Situation I would like to deal with	First-stage skills I might use

Second-stage skills

Your child is unlikely to respond positively at all times to your new ways of communicating. This is normal and to be expected. We wouldn't want children to behave like robots who respond on cue at all times. It is unlikely that you, too, will have sufficient self-control, patience and determination not to revert to former ways of engaging cooperation. It isn't easy to change a pattern of relating that may have developed over several years. There will be times, however, when you will be deliberately ignored, or disobeyed, regardless of your appropriate responses and your calm, assertive manner.

Be prepared for some disappointment and frustration and recognise that different skills are necessary on these occasions. What kinds of response work best when children deliberately misbehave? Many mothers feel that punishment of some kind, either a smack or other negative consequence will best ensure cooperation. Punishment may result in a temporary control of the situation but may well make things more difficult in the future.

How can punishing a child make the situation worse for you and your child?

Some children use bad behaviour to gain control or to gain attention; punishment gives them the attention they crave. Even though the attention given is negative, it is preferable in the child's eyes to what they perceive as inadequate attention from you. If you punish a child you are fuelling his attention-seeking behaviour and the more he is punished the more he will repeat his misbehaviour. You can soon find a child's misbehaviour taking up a disproportionate amount of your time and emotional energy as you strive to find a punishment that will work. Can you identify with the mother in the diagram below who is feeling an escalating sense of crisis as she tries in vain to secure cooperation through punishment that isn't working?

Negative Responses

'Amy, please tidy your room now so that I can clean it.'

Thinks – If it's not done within 15 minutes, she'll be punished. If she gets away with one thing, I'll lose control.

Leads to

'Amy this room isn't tidied properly. I'm not interested in your excuses, you're grounded for two weeks.'

Thinks – I know she was in the middle of her homework, but I daren't show any weakness.

Leads to

'Amy, I expect you to do as I say when I tell you, not when you think you will.'

Thinks – If I give an inch, she'll take a mile.

Leads to

'Every time you disobey me, I will punish you.'

Thinks – I'm scared that one day she will refuse to do as I say. I don't know what I would do. Everything would fall apart.

Leads to

133

Children who are punished may feel humiliated, full of hatred, fear, guilt or revenge and develop greater powers of defiance and resistance to your demands for co-operation. You may find that you cannot rely on their cooperation over matters that seemed easy to deal with previously, for example looking after younger children, or being responsible enough to be left alone in the house. This can be particularly frustrating if it involves you in having to reorganise your own working schedule. Worse still is an escalating worry that the children are becoming more, rather than less, difficult for you to cope with as a working mother.

One effect of punishment on children is to teach them the importance of not getting caught; they will repeat the behaviour but only when you are not around! This may make you feel constantly on edge as you worry what they might be doing in your absence.

Punishment fuels the power battle. If children are feeling particularly vengeful, they will find ways of retaliating, learning where you are vulnerable and getting their own back when you are feeling tired and stressed. When this happens, it can be the most devastating experience of your working week. Sometimes you feel you have had enough and may well feel 'I just can't be bothered any more'.

Punishment relies on force and coercion and makes *you* responsible for your child's behaviour. Alternative methods of gaining cooperation are needed that make children, not parents, responsible for their behaviour – methods that give children the opportunity to make their own decisions. How can we help children learn to take responsibility, develop self-control?

Offer alternatives that appeal to them and are helpful to you

When your child's behaviour is causing difficulty, a natural reaction is to draw attention to what she is doing wrong, e.g. don't play that music so loud, stop running away from the trolley, get your hands off that, don't eat like that. We may follow these commands with threats of what might otherwise happen, e.g. you'll not watch TV, be allowed to play out, borrow my car and so on. Often our desperate demands are ignored and may seem to perpetuate the very behaviour we want to eradicate – the child persists in running away from the trolley, the music remains too loud. Steeling yourself not to home in on the misbehaviour (and this does take practice) and focusing instead on the behaviour you *want* is far more effective in promoting change. With a younger child this acts as a distracter, especially if your suggestions are appealing to her. With older children, your emphasis on the positive, no-blame approach, takes away their defensive, retaliatory response and your child is more inclined to cooperate. You both gain.

Example – with a young child

Instead of

'Don't walk on those flowers – how many times do you have to be told to keep on the path?'

Distract/suggest helpful alternatives

'See if you can find any of those pink stones on the path and we'll use them to stick on your garden picture tomorrow.'

Example – with an older child

Instead of

'Your room is disgusting. Look at all your clothes on the floor. Tidy it up or you won't be going out tonight.'

Focus on the behaviour you want

'It would be helpful if you could put your dirty clothes in the basket now so I could get on with the washing.'

The words need to be expressed in a calm and friendly, though authoritative, tone of voice.

If the child refuses to be distracted, or won't engage in helpful alternative behaviour:

Use I-messages showing your strong disapproval, stating what you expect, and explaining how she can put things right

Example:

Instead of

'You are so inconsiderate – just look what you've done to the carpet again. It's stained with orange juice. You've been told time and time again not to walk around with drinks. If you can't do what I want then I won't do what you want. I'm not prepared to take you swimming tomorrow. That might teach you to do as you are told.'

1. State your disapproval

'I'm furious that you've spilled orange juice on the carpet again.'

2. State what you expect

'I expect you to drink in the kitchen as I've asked, and not wander around the house with it.'

3. Say how she can put things right

'The juice needs soaking up with kitchen roll and then get a clean floorcloth and make sure all the stain is removed. When it's dry it will need brushing.'

If this method is successful, you have both gained. The child has been dealt with firmly and assertively but without humiliation or aggression. She has been taught what to do now and in the future to put things right if spills occur. She is far less likely to wander around with juice because she has had to deal with the consequence of her action. You feel calm and in control because you have avoided unnecessary arguing and ensured that her misbehaviour has not resulted in extra work for you.

BUT if it happens again:

Give your child a choice

'You can either drink your orange juice in the kitchen or you can have water instead. You decide.'

BUT if it happens again:

Take action and allow the child to experience the consequences of her misbehaviour

Daughter: *'Mum there's no orange juice.'*

Mother: *'Yes, that's right. For the time being you will have to drink water because I am not prepared to have orange juice spilt on the carpet. You may decide again what you want to do at the end of next week.'*

This way of disciplining children has real advantages over punishment:

It holds the children not the parent responsible for their behaviour.
It lets the children decide on their course of action.
It lets children learn from the consequences of their behaviour.

Some consequences arise naturally – the child who decides not to wear his wellington boots gets wet feet, the teenager who hands course work in late gets in trouble. Other consequences, although just as clearly related to the behaviour, may have to be explained so that your child can see that they 'fit' what he has done or not done. For example, the child who repeatedly turns up late for the family meal learns he must make do with sandwiches that he can prepare himself. The child who wears his best coat out to play has to wear it later with mud all over it or use his pocket money to have it cleaned. It is often difficult as a working mother to let your child experience the consequence of his behaviour because you believe it will be worse for you in the long run. So, you may run after the child who has forgotten his dinner money, allow the children to watch a TV programme that was conditional on their doing a chore still not done, and feel compelled to take charge of wakening a child who persistently ignores her wake-up call, believing it saves time and rows.

A typical problem for many working mothers is the early morning drama – getting children up, making sure everyone is dressed, fed and with the day's belongings ready for a specific departure time.

Early morning scenario in one typical family home

Mary takes responsibility for getting her child up. She calls several times without hearing a reply. She goes into the bedroom shouting that Lucy must be up in five minutes or everyone will be late. Finally, in desperation, she pulls the clothes off the bed and pulls Lucy out. Lucy is extremely bad-tempered and she has to be coaxed to eat her breakfast. Mary remembers that it's games today and has to search frantically for Lucy's games shorts, which she eventually discovers under the bed. They finally get into the car, furious with each other. Mary drops Lucy off at the end of the road to catch her bus to school. Lucy is on time for school; Mary is 10 minutes late for work and misses an important telephone call. Lucy doesn't give the morning a thought; Mary is still thinking about it an hour later.

How could Mary change the scenario?

Her first task will be to tell Lucy that the morning routine is going to change and what she expects from Lucy from now on: that Lucy will be in charge of herself for getting up, getting dressed, eating breakfast and having all her things ready to leave by 8.30am.

Allowing her to make choices

Lucy can be given an alarm clock or taught how to set one. Mary must not fuss about breakfast. If the family eat breakfast separately she must let Lucy know that it is up to her to choose whether to eat breakfast or not.

In the same way, if the family eat cooked breakfast together in the morning let Lucy know the choice she must make. If she wants breakfast, then she must be there by 8am dressed and ready for school. If she isn't there Mary will presume she isn't choosing to eat breakfast on that day. Mary must be matter-of-fact about the situation. If Lucy turns up late she may eat an apple, but it is too late for cooked breakfast. If Lucy misses her meal, she will experience the natural consequences of missing breakfast – feeling hungry, and may well decide it's worth making an effort to be on time for breakfast the following day.

Letting her learn from the consequences

If Lucy missed her bus through her lateness, the consequence would be that she would have to walk to school or catch a later bus. Either way she would be late for school. It may be important for Lucy to experience the inconvenience of having to walk to school (if it is within walking distance and not dangerous), or catching the later bus and the consequences of arriving late for lessons.

Teaching her new routines

Mary must encourage Lucy to get her things ready for school the night before. Once in place, this will become a habit for her; children quickly get used to new routines. She must refrain from constantly reminding Lucy about dinner money, PE kit, music lessons, homework, bus fare and so on. Mary has enough to remember without taking responsibility for everyone else's morning routine and diaries. Lucy must learn what it's like to sit out games, borrow money for her meal, go without crisps at break – otherwise she will never learn to take responsibility for herself and will continue to let others do so.

Some things to remember

Actions speak louder than words   Children notice how you behave and can become resentful and confused if your actions don't line up with your words. If you are eating breakfast before getting ready for work, or drinking orange juice in the bathroom, but expecting children to abide by different family rules, they are less likely to be cooperative.

Be kind and firm   Your tone of voice is important. It must reflect an attitude of acceptance and kindness. You may use the right words in dealing with your child, for example, *'I can't work with all that noise; you can choose to turn the TV down or leave the room.'* However, if there is anger and threat in your voice, and your attitude is hostile, you may turn a consequence into a punishment. You are encouraging children to make responsible decisions, not forcing them into submission, and so your tone needs to be matter-of-fact and non-punitive. If you are able to view your child's behaviour objectively and not as a personal affront, you will feel calmer and in control and your tone of voice will reflect this.

Firmness in keeping your word about your intentions and following through with appropriate action is essential if you want your child to learn to take responsibility for his behaviour. Firmness is not the same as strictness; it is an attitude to yourself rather than to your child, to your behaviour, your feelings and your decisions. Making your mind up to be firm and assertive helps you to feel good about yourself and to behave in an appropriate and effective way.

The diagram that follows illustrates what you are likely to be thinking as you follow through with the action that is the logical consequence of Amy's behaviour.

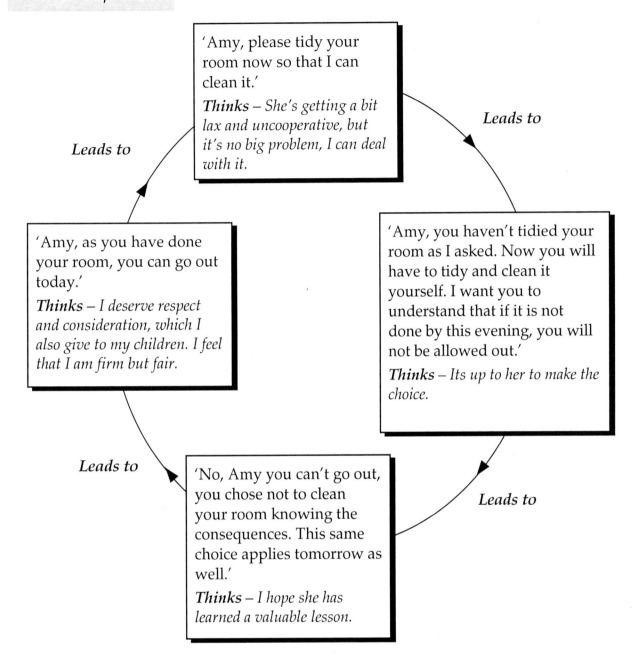

'Amy, please tidy your room now so that I can clean it.'
Thinks – *She's getting a bit lax and uncooperative, but it's no big problem, I can deal with it.*

Leads to

'Amy, you haven't tidied your room as I asked. Now you will have to tidy and clean it yourself. I want you to understand that if it is not done by this evening, you will not be allowed out.'
Thinks – *Its up to her to make the choice.*

Leads to

'No, Amy you can't go out, you chose not to clean your room knowing the consequences. This same choice applies tomorrow as well.'
Thinks – *I hope she has learned a valuable lesson.*

Leads to

'Amy, as you have done your room, you can go out today.'
Thinks – *I deserve respect and consideration, which I also give to my children. I feel that I am firm but fair.*

Leads to

Children will push you to change your mind about carrying out the planned action and you may be tempted to succumb to the pressure and go back on your word. Try not to do this. You are not in contest about winning and losing; your aim is to help your child become responsible for her behaviour. If you give in to your child, she doesn't learn to take the consequences. (She learns instead that if she goes on and on at you long enough, you will give in.) You will not benefit from changing your decision. You may feel annoyed with your own weakness, and cross with her for pushing you to change your mind. The arguments and badgering will be greater next time and you may feel even more stressed and ineffective. There is no need to fight. Keep talking to a minimum and don't engage in argument. Calmly and clearly state your intention. *'I'm sorry Jill, you knew your share of the work had to be finished before you'd be allowed to watch TV at 8pm. You haven't finished it so you'll have to miss the programme.'*

If necessary leave the room where the conflict is taking place so she cannot engage you in further argument. Whatever happens, *refuse to fight about it*. Your child may whine on – *'But Mum, I've been waiting all week to see this ...'* Keep your response calm and firm. *'No Jill, our agreement was that you would finish the work before 8pm. It isn't finished so you'll have to miss the programme.'*

Third-stage skills

When a problem persists you may need to apply more complex skills to deal with the situation. You feel you have tried everything. You are at your wit's end because you find the problem is preying on your mind, intruding into your work and your leisure time. You will need to adopt a problem-solving approach with her, working together to come up with a solution that suits both of you. The most difficult task is to accept that your attitude to the problem needs to shift from seeing it as a 'problem' she owns, to seeing it as something going wrong in the relationship – something you both need to work on. It is so difficult to make this shift. When she has been causing difficulties for you, making your life as a working mother almost impossible, you may have reached the stage when you see coercion and punishment as the only answer. You have a secret worry that if you are not strict enough, she will take advantage and things will deteriorate even more. It is difficult, too, to give up the idea that you have the right answer; you both need to agree on the answer or things will not improve for either of you. Think of this not as a contest in which there is a winner and a loser, but as a problem-solving situation that you are working on together to find a solution where you both win.

Steps in using a problem-solving approach

1. Do not try to problem-solve at the time the problem behaviour occurs.

Find a time when you are both feeling calm in a place where you won't be interrupted, maybe when you are in the car or having a meal together. Check that your child wants to talk about things. If he refuses, write a note following the same steps as suggested below.

2. Talk about your child's feelings.

Example 1

'I've been thinking that it must be irritating for you to be shouted at to get up every five minutes in the morning and to be blamed for our lateness in getting off to school.'

140

Example 2

'I've been thinking that it must be a pain having me go on about your homework all the time, when your teachers are on at you too.'

Wait for a reply – by talking about your child's feelings first, you engage his interest.

3. Explain how *you* feel

Example 1

'I get frustrated when I call you and you don't take any notice, because I'm concerned I'll be late for work.'

Example 2

'I worry that you'll get behind with your school work when you spend so little time on homework.'

Keep this part of your discussion short even though you may be dying to launch into a prima donna performance of how you are feeling.

4. List all possible solutions contributed by *both* of you.

Write down anything and everything that comes to mind no matter how bizarre. Try to start with contributions from your child first and don't comment positively or negatively on the suggestions.

Possible list for Example 1
Call without shouting
Buy a new alarm clock
Get a clock radio
Get up the first time of being called
Get Dad to wake me
Use a bike for school
Ring a bell
Book an alarm call

Possible list for Example 2
Have a homework list for the week
Do homework before tea
Let me decide when to do homework
Have a completed homework diary
Don't do any homework
Have a new desk
Get a new computer
Do homework at school
Work with a friend
Have a homework-free night each week

5. Together decide which ideas you can both agree on.

Cross off ones with which either of you are uncomfortable. In discussion use 'I' statements rather than critical ones.

For example say, *'I'm afraid our finances won't run to a computer, more's the pity,'* rather than, *'A computer is out of the question, you know we can't afford anything like that.'*

(It may happen that you can't find a solution that you can both agree on, but nothing is lost. You have discussed things together amicably and maybe, for now, it's the best you can hope for. You have made some headway and next time you may find a solution that you can agree on.)

When you have both agreed on what would work:

6. Develop an action plan.

It is vital that you plan who is going to do what and when it is going to start, and make a date for follow-up discussion to see how the plan is working.

It is important that your child sees himself as an important part of the solution rather than, as previously, the cause of the problem.

You may not necessarily have to follow this plan step by step. The difficulties may be resolved without Step 4 for instance: you may agree on the way forward without needing to write things down. If the plan works for a while and then goes wrong, be determined to work out another solution together. It may test your patience now, but it is well worth it in the long run. Remind yourself that there is nothing more draining on the emotions, energy and time of a working mother than an uncooperative child.

After reading this section on encouraging cooperation, go back over conflicts you have experienced with your child, analyse what happened and work out an alternative strategy for the future.

Questionnaire on dealing with conflict situations with your child

Think of a situation to which you recently responded aggressively

Describe the situation

What were your needs in the situation?

What were your child's needs in the situation?

Describe how you reacted (write down your words, your feelings and your behaviour).

Describe how your child reacted. Write down her words, her feelings and behaviour

Describe the immediate outcome

Predict the long-term outcome

What did you learn?

What did your child learn?

Describe an alternative that would allow you both to feel OK

What steps could you take to avoid the situation happening again?

Encouraging independence and self-reliance

One of the most effective ways of making your life as a working mother more relaxed and rewarding for you and your family, is to help your children become less dependent on you and more confident and skilled in doing things for themselves. As children learn to do things for themselves and make decisions without constantly seeking your opinion or approval, you are gradually freed from managing the details of each child's life and have more opportunity to share quality time with them. To achieve this you must be prepared to let children take on some of the tasks you have always done for them, let them work out their own solutions to their problems and allow them to learn from their own mistakes. This is not an easy task! When you are rushing out of the house at 8am with children in tow or trying to prepare the family meal in half an hour, it seems so much easier to do things yourself. If you find children struggling with a task, worried about a relationship, wondering which choice to make, it seems kinder and less time-consuming to give instant advice and quick answers to their problems. What is wrong with giving children the benefit of your experience? You know what works best. But by doing too much for children, offering ready-made solutions to all their difficulties, you do not give them a chance to learn to take responsibility for their actions or learn the decision-making process.

They may appear to be grateful for your advice or solution to their difficulty at the time. However, when people are placed in dependent positions, they are also likely to experience feelings of helplessness, resentment, frustration and even anger. Can you remember any occasion when a member of your family, or a colleague at work, took over a task you were doing because they believed they were quicker or more skilled than you were? How did you feel? Or have you had the experience of being told by other people (who were convinced they knew better than you) which type of

145

career would suit you best or which people you should or should not socialise with? How did you feel? It's probably accurate to say you would not like your children to feel this way towards you. So helping your children to function more confidently on their own will not only make your lives far easier, it will also enhance their self-esteem and strengthen your relationship with them.

There are so many occasions when resourceful and independent children are a real bonus for busy working mothers – able to work things out for themselves, get themselves organised in the morning rush, take responsibility for what they need when you are desperate for time, being used to meeting other people and socialising easily, having the ability to cope with the unexpected when you are unavoidably delayed or have made different arrangements for them. Many of the working mothers in our survey reported a growing sense of responsibility in their children as a bonus of their working and of their efforts to encourage independence.

How can you encourage independence and self-reliance?

The opportunities you have to encourage your child's independence by using the skills listed below present themselves every day.

- ◆ Offer children choices
- ◆ Allow children time to find their own answers
- ◆ Give children appropriate responsibility
- ◆ Teach children safety
- ◆ Acknowledge and encourage children

Offer children choices

One of the most effective ways to encourage independence is to offer choices to your children. The ability to choose gives children a sense of control over issues that directly concern them. They begin to build up confidence in their own taste; they learn to seek options, to weigh up alternatives and to predict how their choices will work out. If they then experience the consequences of their decision they learn that their choices have real impact on their lives.

How do you rate as a choice giver? Complete the exercise that follows.

For *each* of the following areas, list those choices you regularly allow your child to make.

Personal appearance:

Clothes:

Furnishing of own room:

Household chores:

Friends:

School activities:

Leisure activities:

Holiday activities:

Family activities:

Food:

Rules:

Pets:

Goals:

If you found difficulty in coming up with examples of choices you allow your child to make in each of the examples, it may mean you are not making use of many of the choices that are available to you and your child.

Allowing children choices saves you time and energy in the long run

Many working mothers with busy schedules say that it saves time and energy if they, rather than their children, decide on such issues as clothes to be worn, food for the lunchbox, or chores to be done. However, in the interest of convenience at the time, you may find that depriving children of choice when they are younger means they gain little practice in learning this essential skill. They may continue to rely on you for direction into their teens and beyond and make increasing demands on your time and energy as more difficult choices have to be made. We all know adults who seem incapable of making decisions for themselves! They become overwhelmed with their options, dependent on others to choose, and are panic-stricken when pushed for an answer.

Allowing children choices encourages commitment and initiative

Giving children choices really benefits your relationship with them. If you order your child to do something for you, he is committed to doing whatever you ask while you are around to enforce the order. By offering a choice, of which chore to do for example, you reduce resistance and encourage cooperation and negotiation. Children find having a choice very motivating and, having decided on an option, are far more committed to carrying out the chore.

Many situations present opportunities for choice

You cannot offer children choices about everything and need to take your child's age and ability into consideration, naturally enough. However, every day there are countless opportunities to let her choose. The way you present choice to her doesn't need to involve you in long-winded discussion. Start with yes-no options: 'Would you like an apple?', or make the choice a simple one. Instead of 'Here's your milk' ask 'Do you want milkshake or plain milk?'. Other simple choices may include, 'Do you want to do your homework before or after tea?', 'Do you want to clean out the car before I take it to town or afterwards?', 'Do you want to wear your brown shorts or your blue ones?'. It is often more expedient to decide things for your child but do remember she needs practice. She also needs structure in learning to choose with confidence. Be specific about the choices and limits: 'Which of these three books do you want me to read?'; 'Could you chose by tomorrow which four friends you want to come to tea on Saturday?'.

Involve your child in more complex choices

Gradually move into offering choices that demand greater evaluation: 'What would you like to buy with your Christmas money?'. As your child's decision-making skills improve, offer more complex planning and decision-making opportunities. You can be quite creative, letting her come up with her own alternatives and offering opportunities to negotiate: 'We have to share out the household chores – how do you suggest we do this fairly?'.

Allow children time to find their own answers

Busy working mothers can very easily fall into the trap of stepping in to 'fix' things, from the puzzle that 'won't work' to the 'lost' T-shirt, the pen that 'won't write', the homework that is 'impossible', the computer file that vanished. If things are fixed by 'wonder mum', children miss the opportunity to resolve their own difficulties and lose out on important learning experiences. We are not suggesting that you do not help your child, rather that you do not automatically take over as soon as there is a difficulty.

It does take real determination and good self-knowledge on our part not to jump in and fix things. We all love being needed and appreciated and bask in comments like 'I wish I could be as clever as you Mum' and 'Aren't you good at mending things!' and 'Were you always good at art when you were at school?', when we fix the broken kite or draw a horse for art homework. We must recognise, too, that we have to fight against seeing their failure as our failure. Fixing things for children reinforces the idea that they cannot handle things for themselves; we are thwarting their growth towards independence by doing so. Rescuing makes us feel loving, powerful and protective and on many occasions feels the right thing to do. However, protection is often counter-productive. It leads to difficulties for children when they come to handle their own problems in the future and attempts to 'fix' and 'rescue' may have you hopping about from one end of the helping spectrum to the other. Instead of catching up with your own work and interests you will find yourself over-involved in ferrying arrangements, homework, shopping trips, chores and secretarial commitments.

A useful way to help children is to offer information that may help them to 'find' the computer file or make a start on the 'impossible' maths homework. Preface your comments with 'It sometimes helps ...' e.g. to turn the computer off and start again, or 'It may help ...' e.g. to list all the purchases in one column.

Here are some examples to illustrate this:

When a child is struggling to draw a picture

Mother's fix-it comment	Helpful comment
Here, you are taking ages over that. Let me help you.	*It sometimes helps to draw the outline of the hills first.*
Encourages dependency	Encourages self-reliance

When a toddler is trying to put on his own pants

Mother's fix-it comment	Helpful comment
Come and sit on my knee and I'll put them on for you.	*It may help to sit on the floor to put them on.*
Encourages dependency	Encourages self-reliance

When a teenager is trying to write his CV

Mother's fix-it comment	Helpful comment
Let me take it to the office and get it professionally done	*It may help to buy a book that gives ideas on layout*
Encourages dependency	Encourages self-reliance

When a child wants to stay home in order to miss a French test that he is feeling sick and anxious about

Mother's fix-it comment	Helpful comment
Well, you can stay home from school but you'll have to spend the day doing French work.	*Have you thought about letting your French teacher know the problem?*
Encourages dependency	Encourages self-reliance

List some of your child's activities in which you have a tendency to take over.

Activity	Fix-it behaviour
Example When my child tries to knit	I always end up with the knitting on my lap, having picked up dropped stitches and made it look 'neat'

As a working mother you may question why it isn't a good idea to give children the benefit of your motherly advice when they seek answers to a problem situation. The best reason is that if you are seeking to build children's self-reliance there is so much more constructive help to give than instant advice. The trouble is that it feels good to us when we share our wisdom with another person and we are reluctant to relinquish our advice-giving role.

Example

'Mum, John expects me to share my crisps and chocolate bar with him at lunchtime. His mum won't let him bring snacks to school. He has horrible sandwiches and muesli cake. I feel sorry for him 'cos he's my friend but I'm fed up with sharing my snacks. What should I do?'

You may feel like saying:

'Don't take crisps or a chocolate bar in future / Tell him your mother says you aren't to share your lunch / Don't give him any / Eat your lunch with someone else.'

If your suggestion works then the problem is solved. However, next time your son has a difficulty, he's learned that you can be relied on to come up with an answer for him and will no doubt ask you again. The more it happens, the more dependent he will become on you for advice. If the advice does not work then he blames you for the outcome and doesn't learn to take responsibility for his decisions.

What are some of the alternatives to instant advice-giving?

Help him sort out his feelings   *'From what you've been saying, you feel sorry for him because he isn't allowed snacks, but you are cross because he seems to expect to have half of yours every day.'*

Wait for him to continue the conversation.

Restate his problem as a question   *'So the problem is how to keep friends with John without giving him half your snacks every day?'*

Again wait for him to continue the conversation.

Offer your ideas tentatively   If you come up with an option for your child to consider, do so after he has exhausted his ideas and is still stuck for a solution. Introduce your idea as one for his consideration:
'Do you think it would work if you left out the crisps and snacks just for a while?'
Rather than saying:
'Why don't you stop taking crisps and snacks for a while?'

Give your views if you feel strongly about the situation   If you feel it is important for your child to understand your values on a particular issue then make this clear in an 'I' statement:
'It bothers me to think John is eating crisps and biscuits when his mother has told him not to.'

Give children appropriate responsibility

Get children to help with household chores

As working mothers we get so used to doing everything for very young children that it does take real effort to take time to teach, and then to make sure children help as they get older. How much help do you expect from children? One of the mothers in our survey said, *'I have a rule that I never do anything that another member of my family is capable of doing.'* This sounds a rather optimistic goal for most of us to achieve but it is important to make it clear to children exactly what you expect from them. In order to achieve a situation where children expect to contribute to household tasks without too much arguing keep the following points in mind.

Be sure you have the right attitude

If you are successfully to engage your children in sharing the family chores then much depends on your own attitude. If you consider the chores as *your* responsibility then your children will get the idea that they are *helping* you when they tidy up their room or empty the dining room bin. If, however, you consider household tasks as the family's responsibility, then by doing chores children feel that they are contributing to the smooth running of the house. There is a real difference between the messages *'Lay the table for me, that's a good girl'* and *'Could you lay the table: we need to eat before 7pm tonight.'* You may feel that children wouldn't even notice the difference but it is the everyday repetition of the message *do this for me* that gradually influences their view of things. It results in children who think housework is their mother's job and consider they are doing her a favour if they contribute to the chores. If you decide to pay children to do routine household chores you are in effect giving them the same message – *I will pay you to do my work.*

Start early

Young children love to help. All too often we deny them the opportunity to do so because of the resulting mess, chaos and extra work this entails. However, it is vital to make helping a habit from a young age.

Allow children to choose a regular job

The chosen job may be putting out rubbish, setting the table, emptying the dishwasher or walking the dog each day. This then becomes 'their' job. When the boredom sets in, as it inevitably does, it is important that you insist that the job continues to be done. You may wish to negotiate a change of regular job with your child from time to time but getting into the habit of doing something each day towards the family chores is most important.

Keep to your word

If you decide with your daughter that from now on she will hoover her room, then any lapse on your part (*'I did it because I was hoovering upstairs anyway'* or *'It looked a mess and Grandma is coming'*) means the job will become yours once again.

Organise a family rota   As children grow older it makes sense to organise an agreed rota of responsibilities (including all adults on the list) and have regular family meetings to discuss problems and negotiate changes. The rota should be put in a prominent place so everyone knows their own and other family members' responsibilities.

Teach children safety

As children become older, gradually teach them to use, under your supervision, appliances that were previously banned, such as plugging in the electric kettle, lighting the gas, using the toaster or turning on the central heating. Ideally, your children should be well practised in using such appliances before they are allowed to use them when you are not around, so that you will feel confident of their ability when you give them the responsibility.

Teach safety routines   Accidents can happen at any time but by preparing your children for such misfortunes you will ensure that they will know what to do.

Keep a list of emergency numbers by the phone (doctor, police, workplace, friends and neighbours).

Teach simple precautionary things like how to turn the water off at the mains, how to turn off the electricity, how to turn off the burglar alarm, how to use the fire extinguisher, how to leave the house in an emergency. Put this basic information on a chart that is easily consulted.

Teach safety with strangers   You cannot protect children for ever, yet long before they are ready to go out of the house alone, to cross roads, to use public transport, to be alone in the house, you can provide them with knowledge about the dangers that may arise in certain situations. Aim to alert children not to frighten them. Teach children about crossing roads, people awareness, using public transport, knowing the area where they live, rules for being alone in the house which may include not opening doors to anyone or answering the phone; (some working mothers use a special code to let children know they are phoning, such as letting the phone ring four times, putting the phone down and ringing again.)

If you have prepared your children to deal with potential difficulties in this way, you know your children are more likely to be sensible and responsible when you are not around, and this helps you to feel less pressured when you have to be away from home for whatever reason.

Acknowledge and encourage your children

There is a subtle difference between specifically encouraging children and merely praising them. Praise is a positive judgement about your child that emphasises your approval of him and of his behaviour. It is a type of reward that reinforces obedience and people-pleasing, and attempts to motivate children with external rewards, e.g. *'If you do something that I feel is good you will be rewarded by being valued by me.'*

Children learn above all to gain your approval in order to feel good about themselves. Their feelings of worth are dependent on your judgement of them and of their actions – *'What a helpful/clever/well organised/creative girl you are!'*

Recognition and encouragement, on the other hand, focus on the child's actions and the satisfaction he derives from his actions. You don't have to mention how you feel. Your pleasure is not the reason for encouraging him to act in a certain way. Consider these examples and the different message that each response carries for the child.

Example 1

Your child has just completed a difficult task after spending more than the allotted time for homework.

Rather than

'I'm impressed by you; you're really clever.'

The message may be that his being clever depends on succeeding at difficult tasks and you are impressed by him when he is doing so. Is he clever when he tries very hard or gets something wrong? He may think *'I'm not really clever – I was just doing what the teacher told us and it took me far longer than it should.'*

Say

'That showed real determination – it looks as if you really worked hard at that. / You've learned a lot from working that problem through.'

The message is unconditional. It is far more specific, giving feedback on what he has achieved.

Example 2

Your daughter has given a much acclaimed performance at school and gained the music prize.

Rather than

'I am so proud of you.'

Could you be saying you make me look good or I'm so pleased because I've always dreamed of having a talented musician in the family?

Say

'You played your piece so accurately and with such feeling tonight; you must be so proud of getting the prize.'

– specific feedback recognising her skill and the feelings she feels in the achievement.

Example 3

Your daughter has completed a chore you have asked her to do.

Rather than

'What a good girl you are!'

She may not be feeling good at all; in fact she may be feeling quite resentful and cross.

Say

'The kitchen is really clean with the floor swept and all the papers put away. Thanks.'

Your daughter can accept the reality of this and be pleased with herself. Even if she was resentful, you have drawn attention to what she has achieved and this results in her feeling competent.

If you are able to express positive thoughts about your children's behaviour in this way, they will become more confident and self-reliant as they grow increasingly aware and appreciative of their own strengths. They learn to identify and accept what they can and can't do without depending on your opinion. If you have more than one child you may find the children less likely to fight for your approval and attention. Many children, when asked to talk about their strengths at school, are unsure about what they are. However, most would have no difficulty at all in reciting a long list of their weaknesses! Use encouragement to find ways to ensure you help your children to know and appreciate themselves.

Now that you have reached the end of this chapter, you may be feeling more confident about your ability to deal positively with situations that arise with your family. Consequently, you will have more energy to invest in creating greater fulfilment at work. The next chapter is concerned with you and your work.

You and Your Work

This section is concerned with helping you to consider your current and future working life and to take positive steps to achieve your full potential as a working mother, now and in the future.

Consider your reasons for working:

- ◆ financial necessity
- ◆ financial independence
- ◆ to improve your standard of living
- ◆ to be seen as a person in your own right – not as parent or partner
- ◆ to use your talents and skills
- ◆ intellectual stimulation
- ◆ sense of achievement
- ◆ to enjoy a life outside the home with your own friends and colleagues
- ◆ a combination of several factors

Whatever your reasons for working, wherever and however you work, in paid or voluntary work, job-sharing or working from home, we believe that you have real opportunity for gaining greater happiness and fulfilment from your work during these busy years if you give time and consideration to your own personal and professional development.

How being a mother may affect your work

Almost all the mothers who answered our questionnaire took pride in, and enjoyed, their work. This was as true for high-flyers as it was for those mothers working at a part-time or less demanding job, chosen mainly for convenience or to bring in extra money. Many mothers felt they were better at their jobs since they had had children.

Some of the benefits

Being more efficient

A number of women said how much more organised they were since having children, as they had learned to fit so much more into their day. They found they were better at planning, delegating and sorting out the important from the not-so-important in their place of work.

Cathryn: *'Because I want to make sure I leave on time, I am careful to prioritise what needs to be done and decide how long things take. I never did this before having children and I would stay working later without getting much more done than I do now.'*

Jill: *'I find I waste less time now – I don't feel so relaxed though, but I'm certainly better at keeping to deadlines.'*

Being more caring

Several women mentioned the influence of motherhood on their personality, feeling more empathic and mature through their experience of caring for babies and young children.

Eve: *'I have far more patience in dealing with people – if someone makes a mistake or gets annoyed about something.'*

Judy: *'I seem to have become the person who people talk to at work if they are worried.'*

Having a more balanced view of work

Several women said they had a better perspective on work. It no longer played such a dominant role in their lives, and since they had a more relaxed attitude to working they found they performed better all round.

Jo: *'I get less worried when things so wrong at work. I have so much more to worry about at home that only I can deal with, and so work problems become less of a priority for me. I know I don't panic as much about meetings and giving presentations as I used to.'*

Being more committed

Although there is a concern that working mothers may be less reliable in their workplace than men or women without children, this is far from the truth. Although working women put their family's concerns high on their agenda this does not result in a neglect of their work. They often go to extra lengths to be seen as responsible, preparing contingency plans for children's illness and taking holiday or unpaid leave when this is essential. Most working mothers enjoy their work, need the money which it provides and have real commitment to doing a good job. Some mothers in our survey said they went out of their way to prove how reliable they were because they felt their employers expected them to be less responsible about time-keeping and putting in extra work when needed.

Anne: *'I came to work one day when I felt very sick because I worried that if I was away, everyone would think I had taken time off for my child.'*

Sally: *'I usually work extra time if I am asked in advance, because it makes such a difference to the attitude of my boss. It's not often I am asked and it's worth the extra organising because it's important to me to be seen to be committed in this way.'*

Being more enthusiastic
Working mothers in our survey said how important it was for them to have another life outside the home, with friends and colleagues who valued them differently.

They felt refreshed by the change in role from mother to worker and this gave them real impetus to develop new ideas, reorganise routines and so on.

Jan: *'I don't recognise myself sometimes. Since I came back to work, I have a real spring in my step and find I have taken on some of the things that have needed doing for ages.'*

Judy: *'I work part-time and on the days I work, I seem to get more done; the more I do the less tired I am. Sometimes I can't believe I do so much in one day.'*

Some of the drawbacks

Having insufficient time
The lack of time for work was mentioned most frequently as one of the problems of being a working mother.
Although some mothers worked overtime and stayed late if necessary, the majority did not. Deciding what to do when a family or school event clashed with a working commitment was particularly difficult.

Jenny: *'My worst nightmare is having to have something prepared for a particular day because I know I can't work at home with the children around, and if it coincides with my husband being away I get very stressed.'*

Sue: *'I feel very annoyed with some of the people at work because I always leave on time and I know they moan about having to cover for me after 5pm. They don't work out that I am in before them in the morning and have few of my lunch breaks. The majority are men and I think some of them believe I should be at home with my baby – it's very difficult in an atmosphere like this to feel confident.'*

Anne: *'I work at home and I lose out on time because people don't think of it as a 9 to 5 job where I need to put the hours in as if I was working in an office. I get interrupted, asked to look after other children, help out when cars break down, even though I have been quite assertive about my need to work, I do think it isn't easy keeping the space free.'*

Having insufficient energy
Some working mothers in our sample said they hadn't enough energy for their work because of the tiredness which came from looking after young children. Having

159

to cope with a day at work after a sleepless night was very draining.

Jane: *'By the time I have come home after work and collected my baby from my mother, I could quite easily climb into the cot with her and stay there till morning, I feel so worn out.'*

If you have very young children, your energy level is likely to be low but if your tiredness continues when they are sleeping well, it is worth considering how far the job itself is sapping your energy and enthusiasm either because it is too demanding, or too boring.

Having less confidence

Some of the working mothers returning to work after having had a baby, or after a longer career break, initially sought jobs which they could cope with easily and which fitted in with their lifestyle.

Jill: *'When I returned to work, I felt I had aged 10 years though it was only 18 months. I kept my head down and got on with it and could do the job very easily yet I didn't see then that I was wasting my time. It took me a year to get my confidence back.'*

Are you giving time and energy to your own professional development?

Many working mothers neglect their career development during their busiest family years. Ask yourself how much time and energy you have invested in the development of your career over the last few years? Think about the time, money and effort you have put into your home, your financial planning, your children's education, your holidays and leisure activities and compare this with the time, money and effort you put into your own professional development. What does your comparison tell you? Probably that you are investing too little time and energy in the management of your own career! Yet during these years when you are rushing around like a hurricane you will make decisions about your career that will affect the rest of your life. These important decisions should be made thoughtfully and deliberately with real awareness of the kind of life and career you would find most satisfying. The majority of working mothers in our survey felt they gave little *strategic* thought to their career management.

What women told us

Julie: *'I'm sure I could do something that would suit me better, but I don't have any idea of what that might be.'*

Sally: *'The job I have now fits in well with the children and that's my main concern when they are little. I can't say I think about my future career much.'*

Eve: *'I never have the energy to think about five years' time. I'm busy getting on with today.'*

Sue: *'My husband's job pays more than mine and we've always moved for his work. I usually wait until I see what's available in the new place.'*

Some women, like Joy, felt: *'I only do it for the money – the job's boring.'*

160

Others in contrast, like June, loved their work: *'This job is great. I worry that the company will close because without this work I would be lost.'*

Angela: *'I love my work as a part-time doctor, but I don't think about where I go from here.'*

Judy worried: *'I haven't got the qualifications I need to get a well-paid job.'*

A common view was expressed by Anne: *'I'm planning to do something different when the children are all at school.'*

If you consider how much difference a challenging, fulfilling and enjoyable career can make to your happiness and prosperity and how it can influence the well-being of your entire family, you may feel that it is worth investing more time and energy in your own professional development. You owe it to yourself to recognise and realise your full potential. Start planning *now* to give yourself the best chance of success. You need to be proactive in shaping your career to fit your needs and be ready to take opportunities as they arise, rather than reacting to changes in your work situation without any previous thought or preparation.

Life and career planning

You may find it useful to write down your answers to the following questions to help you think ahead about your life and career plans.

At what age did you have your first child? ....

At what age did you have / do you expect to have your last child? ....

What age were you / will you be when your last child started/starts primary school? ....

What age were you / will you be when your last child started/starts secondary school? ....

What age were you / will you be when your last child left/leaves secondary school? ....

What age were you / will you be when your last child started/starts higher education? ....

And finally, what age will you be when your last child is likely to leave home permanently? ....

Now complete the following statements:

♦ Childcare will be a major everyday concern taking a high percentage of my time and energy from when I am .... years until I am .... years.

♦ Childcare will be still a concern but not so demanding from .... years until I am .... years.

♦ There will be only minor issues concerning childcare by the time I am ....

♦ By the time I am .... years, my children will have left home.

♦ I have .... years when I hope to be working in a satisfying career with fewer family commitments.

Investing in your career

Making an investment in your career and professional development involves the same steps as making an investment in other things; you find out about the product, research the market, consider the options available, then make a decision based on your findings. Having purchased your chosen product, you make sure you maintain it. In your career management your investment is in yourself and your care and maintenance needs to be a continuous process.

Make a contract with yourself to spend a certain amount of time and effort managing your career on a regular basis. Be business-like about it. Make sure you buy a large file with plenty of paper and dividers, or create a file **My career development** on the computer.

You may think you have no need for career management as you are not interested in embarking on a new career in a new field with a new set of people; the prospect seems too daunting. However, career management is about helping you to make the most out of your current employment just as much as it is concerned with helping you to consider different occupations and career moves.

Find out about yourself

Self-knowledge is the foundation of a successful career. It is critical to know your range of skills, your strengths and weaknesses, to be aware of your values and personal qualities in order to make realistic career choices, target suitable fields and sell yourself to current or potential employers. Many of us could fulfil more of our potential if we were fully aware of our talents and had the opportunity to use them in our work.

Identify your skills

The first step is to identify your skills and appreciate their worth. A skill is an ability to do something. Your range of abilities is probably far wider than those acknowledged in your current workplace. Many of us take for granted the skills that we use informally and every day, thus remaining unaware what else we could contribute.

The questionnaire that follows will help identify your natural skills. Work through the statements, rating each item on a scale 0-4, noting your score in the box provided. Try to use the entire range of scores and consider the statements in the context of home, work and leisure (don't restrict your thoughts to work). Score your answers as follows:

Very good = 4 points. Moderately good = 3 points. Only fair/adequate = 2 points. Not so good = 1 point. Poor = 0 points.

Skill	Category	Score
Making relationships with others, working with and through others	B	☐
Learning, retaining or remembering information	D	☐
Being creative and innovative, able to come up with new ideas	A	☐
Designing useful objects	C	☐
Communicating clearly and effectively in speech with others	B	☐
Negotiating with individuals or groups	B	☐
Following instructions, diagrams or plans	D	☐
Using hand tools and power tools	C	☐
Managing money, producing accounts, budgeting	D	☐
Developing, adapting and extending ideas	A	☐
Relating to a wide range of people	B	☐

Continues on next page

Skill	Category	Score
Taking an inventory	D	
Improvising, adapting things	C	
Communicating clearly and effectively in writing	A	
Persuading, influencing and motivating others	B	
Being skilful in working with your hands, having manual dexterity	C	
Being aware of how people are feeling and being able to show understanding/intuition	B	
Teaching, training, explaining things	B	
Working creatively with spaces, shapes or patterns, e.g. designing, sketching	A	
Working out why things don't function properly	C	
Being able to pull out the main ideas in a written document	A	
Analysing and classifying information	D	
Being able to be open with people and express your feelings	B	
Thinking quickly and being flexible	A	
Repairing things	C	
Having a logical approach to situations	A	
Noticing differences and inconsistencies in ideas and opinions	A	
Calculating and computing	D	
Having good hand-to-eye coordination	C	

Skill	Category	Score
Evaluating other people's ideas and opinions	A	☐
Assembling, making or building things	C	☐
Being a leader or organiser of others	B	☐
Gathering information by studying or researching	D	☐
Applying knowledge and skills in a new way, being imaginative	A	☐
Finding out and understanding how things work	C	☐
Giving help and support to others	B	☐
Interpreting statistical reports	D	☐
Handling things with precision and speed	C	☐
Carrying out written procedures methodically	D	☐
Handling and manipulating data	D	☐

Add up your scores for each category, A,B,C, and D, and enter your results in the boxes below.

Skill	Category	Score
Ideas	A	
People	B	
Objects	C	
Information	D	

Your scores show where your natural abilities lie, regardless of whether you're making the most of these in your current role. Check the balance of skills between each area: you may have skills in each category but does one area dominate? Your areas of strength will tell you, in general, the type of work in which you are likely to perform best. You need to consider how far these skills are transferable from home to paid work or from one occupation to another. Running a home involves organisational skills (organising family appointments, holidays, social activities, meals etc.), financial skills (paying bills, negotiating with bank managers, budgeting saving etc.) and communication skills (teaching/negotiating with children, dealing with work people etc.). You need to identify these transferable skills because you may well underrate their importance in your career development.

In the transferable skills identification exercise that follows,

1. Put a mark against the statements which describe any skill you have and use.

2. Give it a second mark if you enjoy using these skills.

3. Give it a third mark if it is especially important for you.

Add any skills that are not mentioned in the appropriate place on the diagram.

Identify your favourite transferable skills (the ones with three marks).

Have you got more going for you than you thought?

Are these skills from one ability area?

Are these skills which you use in your current/previous work?

Are these skills which you had not considered to be important before?

Transferable skills identification

Skills with people – in groups

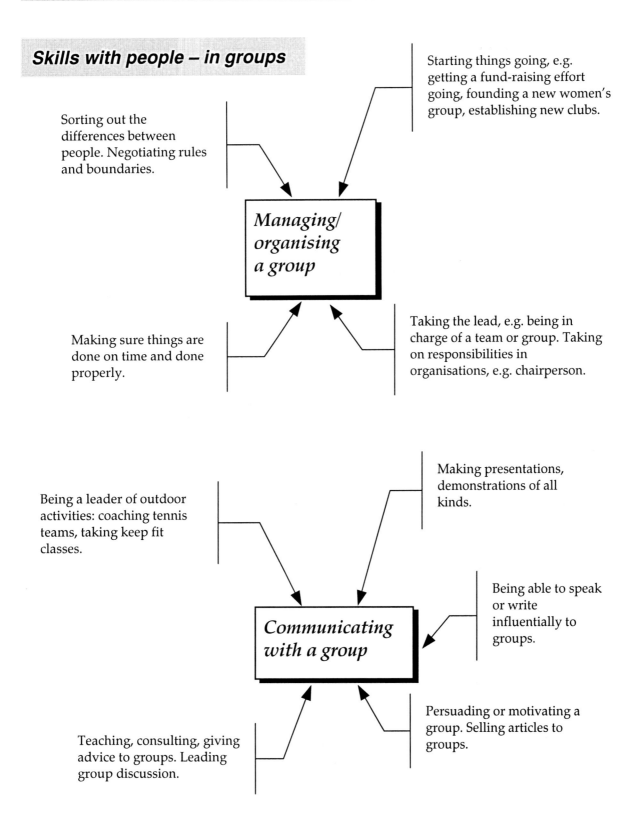

Starting things going, e.g. getting a fund-raising effort going, founding a new women's group, establishing new clubs.

Sorting out the differences between people. Negotiating rules and boundaries.

Managing/ organising a group

Making sure things are done on time and done properly.

Taking the lead, e.g. being in charge of a team or group. Taking on responsibilities in organisations, e.g. chairperson.

Making presentations, demonstrations of all kinds.

Being a leader of outdoor activities: coaching tennis teams, taking keep fit classes.

Being able to speak or write influentially to groups.

Communicating with a group

Teaching, consulting, giving advice to groups. Leading group discussion.

Persuading or motivating a group. Selling articles to groups.

Skills with people – individuals

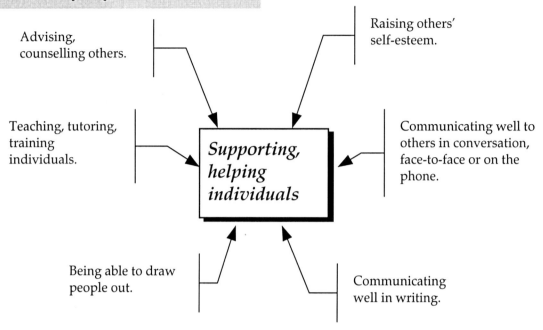

Advising, counselling others.

Raising others' self-esteem.

Teaching, tutoring, training individuals.

Supporting, helping individuals

Communicating well to others in conversation, face-to-face or on the phone.

Being able to draw people out.

Communicating well in writing.

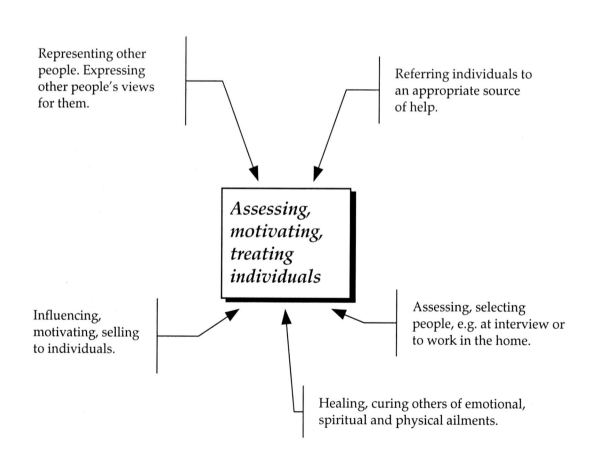

Representing other people. Expressing other people's views for them.

Referring individuals to an appropriate source of help.

Assessing, motivating, treating individuals

Influencing, motivating, selling to individuals.

Assessing, selecting people, e.g. at interview or to work in the home.

Healing, curing others of emotional, spiritual and physical ailments.

Dealing creatively with shapes or spaces.

Inventing, creating or designing new

Acting.

Creating, innovating, experimenting

Conveying thoughts and feelings in a painting or drawing.

Creative writing, e.g. poetry, novels.

Composing music.

Creative dressmaking, working creatively with colour.

Being intuitive, e.g. as in predicting consequences.

Separating important from unimportant, e.g. as when dealing with multiple problems.

Collecting information by studying, reading or researching.

Analysing, researching

Being able to analyse a situation quickly and accurately.

Adapting, translating, developing, improving projects.

Developing other people's ideas.

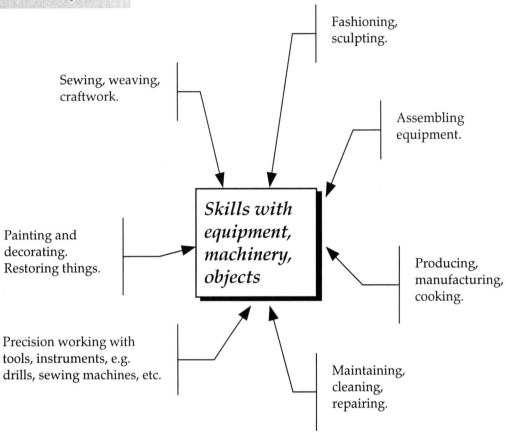

Fashioning, sculpting.

Sewing, weaving, craftwork.

Assembling equipment.

Painting and decorating. Restoring things.

Skills with equipment, machinery, objects

Producing, manufacturing, cooking.

Precision working with tools, instruments, e.g. drills, sewing machines, etc.

Maintaining, cleaning, repairing.

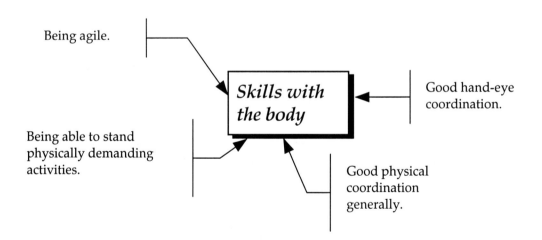

Being agile.

Skills with the body

Good hand-eye coordination.

Being able to stand physically demanding activities.

Good physical coordination generally.

Skills with information

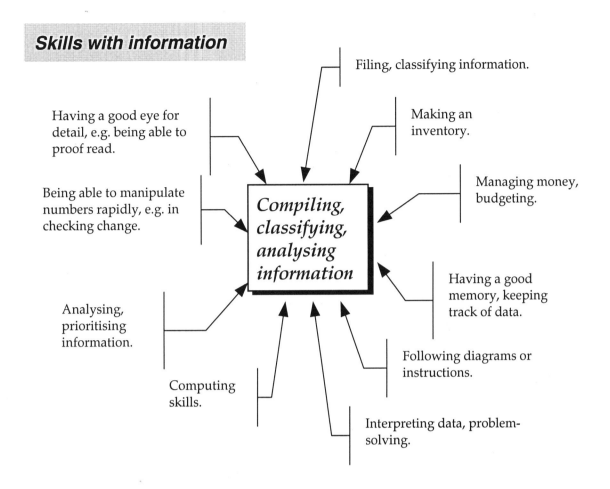

Filing, classifying information.

Making an inventory.

Having a good eye for detail, e.g. being able to proof read.

Managing money, budgeting.

Being able to manipulate numbers rapidly, e.g. in checking change.

Compiling, classifying, analysing information

Having a good memory, keeping track of data.

Analysing, prioritising information.

Following diagrams or instructions.

Computing skills.

Interpreting data, problem-solving.

Identify the personality characteristics that influence your career development

How do you relate to others? How do you deal with tasks? How do you feel about yourself? The more you know about yourself the more you are able to change and develop your career in directions that bring greater happiness and fulfilment. You may be in a work situation currently where you cannot be yourself, or express your personality. You may be coping with work that demands personal qualities you cannot offer. For example, your job may demand efficiency and assertion, which are not your strong points, rather than creativity and imagination where you do have strengths. The more you know and understand yourself the easier it is to make choices that are right for you. The exercises that follow will help you to identify the personal characteristics that are important to consider for your career development and the type of work situation in which you would feel most fulfilled.

Scan the list of adjectives on the following chart, marking those that are like you and crossing out those that are unlike you. Some you may wish to leave blank. Add others that you think are important in making your choice.

Adaptable	Curious	Impractical	Persistent
Adventurous	Decisive	Influential	Powerful
Agile	Down-to-earth	Insightful	Practical
Ambitious	Efficient	Introspective	Quiet
Analytical	Emotional	Kind	Relaxed
Assertive	Empathic	Matter-of-fact	Reliable
Cautious	Energetic	Methodical	Reserved
Changeable	Excitable	Meticulous	Resilient
Charming	Expressive	Modest	Responsible
Cheerful	Frank	Non-conforming	Self-confident
Creative	Generous	Objectives	Sociable
Competitive	Gentle	Organised	Studious
Conforming	Genuine	Original	Tactful
Conscientious	Idealistic	Outgoing	Unconventional
Cooperative	Imaginative	Perceptive	Warm

Go through the list a second time and put a ring around any characteristics that you feel best describe you. Try to choose six to put on your list. (Remember to add your own if they don't appear on the list.)

Personality characteristics that describe me best

1
2
3
4
5
6

Place each word on your list in the appropriate space below (not necessarily in any order). Now consider whether people at home would describe you like this. Mark the appropriate column for their likely response.

	Personality characteristics	People at home would describe me like this			
		Always	Frequently	Occasionally	Never
1					
2					
3					
4					
5					
6					

Ask family or friends whether or not they agree with your evaluation of their response. Are you surprised by any differences in perception? Can you learn anything from this. Jot down any ideas that you have.

Now do the same exercise in relation to yourself at work. Again, place each word on your list in the appropriate space and consider whether or not people at work, now or previously, would describe you like this. Tick the appropriate column for their likely response.

	Personality characteristics	People at work would describe me like this			
		Always	Frequently	Occasionally	Never
1					
2					
3					
4					
5					
6					

Ask people at work whether or not they agree with the evaluation of their response. Are you surprised by any differences in perception? Can you learn anything from this. Jot down any ideas that you have.

Situations in which you feel able to be yourself

Keeping in mind the personality characteristics you have just identified, reflect now on two situations at home and at work (now or previously) when you are/were able to be yourself.

Situations at *home* when I am able to be myself:

Situation 1

Situation 2

174

Situations at *work* when I am able to be myself:

Situation 1

Situation 2

Reflect now on two situations at home and at work (now or previously) when you feel/felt constrained and unable to be yourself.

Situations at *home* when I feel constrained and unable to be myself.

Situation 1

Situation 2

Situations at *work* when I feel constrained and unable to be myself.

Situation 1

Situation 2

Is there a *pattern* in your answers? Can you see in what situations you feel at ease and can be yourself? Which situations make you feel uncomfortable and unable to express yourself?

What is your personal working style?

Below are a number of statements that describe some of the ways in which you may feel, act, or react in work situations (*now or previously*).

Score the statements on a scale 1–10, 10 denoting a statement that is very true for you and 1 one that is least true for you.

1. Read through all the statements picking out approximately 10 that most clearly describe you in work situations and give these statements a very high score (9 or 10).

2. Read through the statements picking out approximately 10 that are least descriptive of you in a work situation and give these a low score (1 or 2).

3. Carry on marking the remainder of the statements with scores which reflect their relevance for you. Try to use the range of scores 3, 4, 5, 6, 7 and 8 for the remaining statements.

4. Add up the scores for each of the letters from (a) to (e) and put the total score against the relevant letter in the space provided after the questionnaire.

		Score
(b)	I can always tell if someone likes me or not	☐
(a)	People tell me that I can take a joke	☐
(e)	If it takes five minutes to get to a place or meeting I allow five minutes	☐
(d)	People who are careless or have a 'take it or leave it' attitude get me down	☐
(c)	I tend to start things then gradually my interest fades	☐
(a)	My feelings are not easily hurt	☐
(b)	I often find myself listening to other people's stories even though I've heard them before	☐
(e)	I am always thinking about the next thing to do before I have finished the present job	☐

(d)   I don't easily admit I can't do things

(c)   Sometimes I get bogged down in the details of a task

(a)   I like to use rational arguments in all situations

(e)   I often get on with a job and leave discussion about it until later

(d)   I often tell people how things should be done rather than letting them get on with it

(b)   I usually do what someone else wants to do rather than insist on what I'd prefer to do

(c)   I put a lot of effort into things but don't get enough done

(a)   Even though I'm over working I can still cope easily with most things, e.g. deadlines, difficult people

(e)   I don't like planning. I'd rather get on with things and see how it works out

(b)   I find it hard to refuse people's requests

(c)   When the end of a project is in sight I sometimes feel uneasy

(d)   I like to be sure that words are spelt correctly

(b)   I go out of my way to win a person's friendship if they seem off-hand

(a)   I'm usually the last to complain about things

(d)   I don't like doing things twice so I make sure they are right the first time

(c)   Although I plan things thoroughly, things don't get done as quickly as I expect

(e)   If I have a lot to do, I tend to get more things done

(b)   I feel uneasy if people criticise me, even if it's not my fault

Continues on next page

(d)   I don't like people correcting me, or making excuses for me

(a)   People who make a fuss and get emotional irritate me

(e)   I sometimes lose my patience with people who are slow

(c)   People who rush to finish things annoy me

(e)   I don't really have enough time to relax

(a)   If someone gets emotional I usually make a joke or tell them to snap out of it

(d)   I am often critical of my work even though it is well done

(b)   I'm not good at telling people what I want

(c)   I put a lot of energy into most things I do

(d)   I like to get things properly done even though it takes longer than I expected

(a)   People tell me that I can take a lot

(b)   I'm not really comfortable with people until I am sure they really like me

(e)   I'm always doing things at the last minute

(d)   I'd rather do something myself then delegate it and risk an inferior job

(c)   Difficult tasks don't bother me – I have plenty of energy for things

(b)   I don't ask people to do things for me very often

(a)   I can keep calm even though other people are showing strong emotions

(e)   I often interrupt people and finish sentences off for them

Score

(b) I spend time thinking about how my decisions will affect other people before deciding on something

(a) I don't like people fussing around me when I'm ill, tired or miserable

(c) Before I start on something I like to do a thorough investigation of possibilities

(e) I often talk too quickly

(d) I'm very quick to see how people could improve on things

(c) I don't like finishing things

	Total score	Put in order of preference
A		
B		
C		
D		
E		

It is likely that you will have two categories with a high score and one category which has a distinctly lower score than the others. This is the most common pattern but many others are possible. The importance of the questionnaire is not in the score itself but in how you have ordered the categories.

On the next page there is an interpretation of the different categories.

A's You are very capable and dependable in your work and able to make careful balanced decisions without getting flustered and emotional. You have a calm, rational manner too in dealing with people in work and don't get involved in unnecessary social chit-chat. People don't find you approachable because you can appear remote and rather cool at times.

> *Think about*: Opening up to others more and sharing feelings; giving yourself some perks.

B's You spend a considerable amount of your time dealing with other people's needs. You are great to have around if trouble arises because you are prepared to spend time ironing out difficulties and getting people to work together again. You want to please everyone, though, and spend too much time listening to other people's difficulties and consequently neglect your own work. This often means you have to rush your work on occasions through helping others to meet their deadlines!

> *Think about*: Saying 'no' to requests; facing your own feelings; giving people an honest opinion when it's necessary.

C's You work extremely conscientiously and really get to grips with what needs to be done. You never take short-cuts and decisions are well considered and well informed always. You can be rather slow to get on with things and other people may hassle you because you won't make decisions immediately or rush things through. You do find it difficult to be clear of the job in hand.

> *Think about*: Getting things finished more quickly; risking criticism; letting yourself go.

D's You are highly organised and extremely efficient in your work. You are great to have around because you always make sure you do a job well so there is no need to check on your work. You are always able to find things for people, come up with the correct dates for meetings, times for deadlines, etc. Unfortunately other people do not often measure up to your standards and you cannot accept their inefficiency easily. You sometimes spend too long on tasks that don't warrant that much attention.

> *Think about*: Taking some short cuts; challenging your views; meeting more people.

E's You are able to get through a great deal of work in a short time and are the envy of many others who work at half the pace! You are great in meetings where ideas are needed and excellent with work that does not require a lot of detail. Problems occur, however, because you sometimes rush through work, which has to be done again. You also rush other people sometimes, leaving them confused about tasks to be done.

> *Think about*: Sitting down more; reflecting on things; giving yourself a plan.

What are your work values?

Our values are very much determined by our experiences of life. The way we have been brought up, the place we lived in, the education we received, all contribute to the values we hold. Our values change over time as we experience different events, change our view of ourselves and what we want to achieve. What seemed important to us when we first started work may give way to other concerns.

It is important to assess and take account of your values in deciding on your career development because if you hold values that match the job you hold then it is more likely that you will put effort and time into it and feel you belong, and so feel happy and fulfilled. Below there are 32 statements that describe work values. You are to score each statement on a scale of 1 to 6:

> **6** denotes values that are very important to you
> **1** denotes values that are relatively unimportant to you

Do try to use all the numbers 1–6 to help you to differentiate your values. The score itself is not as important as which values you rate higher than others. When you have given yourself a score on each of the statements, add up the scores according to the letter alongside each statement and fill in the total score for each letter in the space provided below the questionnaire. Read the description of the work values and try to work out a rank order (a) to (h).

Work values questionnaire

Score

There would be a lot of variety in what I do. ☐ (a)

There would not be any interference from others with my work. ☐ (b)

People would depend on me to come up with answers, take decisions. ☐ (c)

I would be able to earn a high salary. ☐ (d)

My work would be of value to others. ☐ (e)

My job would be very secure. ☐ (f)

I would work with a team of people. ☐ (g)

Continues on next page

My work would be seen as important by others. ☐ (h)

I could be my own boss. ☐ (b)

I would be in charge of a team of people. ☐ (c)

My work would contribute to the community. ☐ (e)

I would be covered in the event of sickness or accident. ☐ (f)

The work would not be routine. ☐ (a)

I would have a generous expense account. ☐ (d)

I would get recognition from others for work well done. ☐ (h)

I would make new acquaintances and friends. ☐ (g)

The work would have a superannuation scheme. ☐ (d)

I could help people cope more adequately with their lives. ☐ (e)

Many people would see the outcome of my work. ☐ (h)

I would have support from people at work for personal and/or job-related difficulties. ☐ (g)

I would be meeting different people and going to different places in the course of my work. ☐ (a)

I could decide for myself on my work tasks for the day. ☐ (b)

I would be involved in such things as policy decisions, staff appointments and promotions. ☐ (c)

There would be few demands made on my time and little work-related stress. ☐ (f)

I could work independently of others. ☐ (b)

I could extend my social life through the people I meet at work. ☐ (g)

I would know what I had to do each day and could do it easily. ☐ (f)

I would have the necessary authority to take decisions. ☐ (c)

Bonuses and incentives would be paid for extra work undertaken, or good work achieved. ☐ (d)

I would be involved in further education training for different aspects of my work. ☐ (a)

People would respect me for the job I have. ☐ (h)

My work would be socially useful. ☐ (e)

Total scores

A ☐

B ☐

C ☐

D ☐

E ☐

F ☐

G ☐

H ☐

Turn over for an interpretation of the categories.

A's You need to have variety in what you do and prefer to choose your own times for doing things rather than having a strict routine or regular schedule. Ideally you would like the opportunity to meet a variety of people and travel to different places in the course of your work. Predictable routine jobs would bore you as you need interest to be kept alive by challenge and change.

Keyword: Variety

B's You are looking to be in charge of your own work, not necessarily your own business, although this would suit you. It is important for you to have space to make decisions on your own, decide what hours you'll work and what tasks you'll tackle in the order you want. You don't like people telling you what to do all the time.

Keyword: Independence

C's You like to be in charge of other people and would be happiest in an occupation where you were responsible for the decision-making of a team, deciding not only how and when things should be done, but who should do them. You like other people asking you for ideas and information and easily take responsibility and leadership roles.

Keyword: Authority

D's Your main drive is financial reward. It is very important for you to earn a high salary and you would sacrifice other values, interest, social hours, job satisfaction, in order to achieve this.

Keyword: Economic

E's You want to help people in your work and would be happiest in a job where you felt you were contributing to society in some way.

Keyword: Service

F's You are looking for security in your work, the security of a safe job with regular income that does not make any demands on your social time or cause you any hassle. The more predictable things are the better you like it.

Keyword: Security

G's Friendly contact with people at work is the most important consideration for you. Work means you get the chance to meet new people, opportunities to talk and exchange ideas and the chance to develop your social life.

Keyword: Social

H's You prefer to have a job that other people as well as you see as important. It would not matter whether this job gave you economic, social or occupational status. It is important to have your achievements recognised.

Keyword: Prestige

The order in which you have placed the value categories is significant in telling you about the kind of work you find rewarding.

Try to pick out the most important work values. If you find that you cannot really distinguish between your values you may find it useful to practise answering the following questions and make up others to help you distinguish between values that seem equally important for you.

Practice questions

If you had any choice between and interesting, varied job that didn't give you any status, or one that was prestigious but less varied, which would you choose?

Answer: Variety or Prestige

If you had a choice between a job in which you were helping other people, but your work colleagues weren't very friendly, or one in which the people were friendly but the work was not in any way contributing to society, which would you choose?

Answer: Service or Social

If you had any choice between a job with a high salary where you didn't make any decisions, just got on with things you were told to do, or a job with a moderate salary where you had a good deal of authority, which would you choose?

Answer: Authority or Economic

If you had the choice between a varied job that could disappear next month, or a more routine job that offered real security, which would you choose?

Answer: Variety or Security

If you had the choice between a job that gave you plenty of chance to exercise your authority, but was 9–5 and the work content determined for you, and a job in which your hours and tasks were flexible but you had little influence on policy decisions and no one working for you directly, which would you choose?

Answer: Authority or Independence

It is essential that I have

It is important that I have

I would like to have

Tick the values that are being met in your current employment and underline the ones that are not.

Your life experiences to date

The following exercise helps you to learn about yourself from everything that has happened in your life so far.

Take a large sheet of paper and draw a river that represents your life. Your river may be a long winding river that starts as a small spring and gets wider and more powerful as it flows along! It may be a short, straight river with many waterfalls representing major life events. It may be a wide, gentle meandering river that flows slowly from start to finish.
The size and shape is up to you. Mark ✖ where you are now.

It is very useful to do this exercise with a friend and describe your river to each other.

Mark in the key events, experiences, achievements and qualifications gained from birth to the present day. Make sure you leave plenty of space between the years to add events as you jog your memory. Mark in everything you can remember of significance. Indicate in **red** any events or experiences that were sad, stressful or disappointing in some way.

Indicate in **green** any events or experiences that were happy, illuminating, exciting in some way.

- ♦ Are there themes that link together the sad experiences?
- ♦ Are there themes that link together the happy experiences?

Mark in **black** on your river any major turning points in your life, e.g. moved house, changed schools, marriage, divorce, birth of children.

Consider whether or not you had a choice at these major turning points in your life and if so how you made the choice. How did you cope with these experiences?

Think about your happy and sad experiences and how you coped with these.

Make a short summary about your life so far, basing the summary on your river and noting major achievements and anything you have learned about yourself from examining your happy and sad times. Are there any themes that characterise these experiences?

e.g.   are all sad times concerned with family events?
are all sad times concerned with failure of some kind?

are all happy times concerned with achievements?
are all happy times concerned with the family?

This analysis will help you to identify the vital things in your life and what your motivators might be.

Your career path to date

It may be useful to look in some detail at your working career. Using a separate sheet of paper for each job, make a note of the following information.

- ♦ The title of your job.

- ♦ The nature of the work / the level of responsibility.

- ♦ Part-time or full-time.

- ♦ The name of the company.

- ♦ The dates that you worked there.

- ♦ Why you took the job.

- ♦ Why you left the job.

- ♦ What you enjoyed about the work.

- ♦ What you disliked about the work.

- ♦ Whether or not you would be happy in this job now. (Give reasons.)

When you have completed this exercise for each of your jobs to date, see if you can identify any themes or threads that run through your career path.

Your weaknesses and restrictions

In managing your career development it is essential to acknowledge what your weaknesses and restrictions are. These may be holding you back, slowing you down, or even stopping you from achieving your potential. The word 'may' is chosen deliberately because many of us trap ourselves into believing certain changes and ways forward are outside our control (especially beliefs we have about ourselves).

There are considerable advantages to be gained by examining your negative attributes; by facing up to them, you can begin to assess their real significance in your career development; by fully understanding your limitations you can avoid situations which may make you uncomfortable; knowing your weaknesses may enable you to see them in a different light. Do some positive thinking! Consider your weaknesses as qualities out of balance – as unexploited strengths!

List your weaknesses in the box below.

Weaknesses	Possible strengths of this
Impatience	Enthusiastic. Keen to get on with things.
Disorganisation	Always doing things. Taking on everything. Very committed.

Share your list with two or three other people who know you well to see if they agree.

What is stopping you from developing your career?

You need to consider this carefully because so far in this self-assessment you have not looked at the possible constraints that may prevent you from achieving your goal. The word 'may' is chosen deliberately because many of us trap ourselves into believing certain changes and ways forward are outside our control (especially beliefs we have about ourselves). Look through the following list of restrictions that may hinder you in your career development and cross out those that do not apply. Consider carefully which things are truly obstacles and which you could do something about. You may need to investigate options. For example, many people think they are barred from taking a degree course because they haven't passed A-levels and don't realise that other (job) qualifications are often accepted.

Obstacles	I can do something about this (list ideas)	I must accept this and think of alternatives (list ideas)
Lack of qualifications		
Lack of skills		
Lack of confidence		
My beliefs about myself		
The unsocial hours demanded by the work		
Full-time commitment is necessary		
Too old		
Lack of money/grant		
Unwillingness to leave local area		
Lack of support from other people		
Family ties/commitment		
Lack of mobility		
Too much competition		
Unwillingness to study		

Having completed the exercises about yourself and your career in this section you should be in a better position to know

♦ what you have to offer

♦ what you want and need

♦ what you are able to achieve

Summary of your findings about yourself

Mark your choice or insert information where appropriate.

My most important skills are with:

People		Information	

	Ideas		Objects

The transferable skills that I identified as important to me are:

Personality characteristics that best describe me and that I want to use in my work are:

My personal working style could be described as:

My predominant work values are:

Variety	Independence
Authority	Economic
Service	Security
Social	Prestige

My achievements / qualifications include:

Experiences in my personal and professional life that I might draw on in my career development include:

Constraints that I have to consider include:

Constraints that I could do something about include:

Are you in the right job?

Knowing more about yourself will help you to consider the next stage in your career management. You need to think carefully about your current employment and decide whether it is right for you. Does it use your skills and strengths? Does it suit your personality? Does it provide you with the values you feel are important? Is it a helpful stepping stone for your career development? Is it giving you real satisfaction?

Consider the questions below to discover how fulfilled you are in your work. If you're unemployed or returning, answer the questions in relation to your most recent job. Score your answers as follows:

Definitely = 2 points. Occasionally = 1 point. No/never = 0 points.

1. Do you feel stretched and challenged in your current job? ☐

2. Do you have a sense of belonging in your workplace? ☐

3. Outside your job, do you talk with self-respect about your contribution at work? ☐

4. Do you believe colleagues talk positively to others about your contribution? ☐

5. Is the content of your job compatible with your lifestyle? ☐

6. Are you motivated to work beyond what is expected of you? ☐

7. Do you enjoy going to work most days? ☐

8. Do you receive good feedback from others for work you've accomplished? ☐

9. Do you put effort into achieving positive relationships with colleagues? ☐

10. Do you seek courses or further training for your current job? ☐

11. Would you encourage others with similar abilities to seek the type of job you have? ☐

12. Would you be against taking a generous redundancy offer? ☐

13. Is your ideal job similar in any way to your present work? ☐

14. Are you encouraged to seek promotion by your boss or other colleagues? □

15. Do you find others envying you your work? □

16. Does your work make use of most of your talents? □

17. Can you see yourself achieving promotion in the next two years? □

18. Do you seldom need challenges outside work? □

19. Do you often feel excited by the prospect of next week's work? □

20. Do you feel stimulated by the majority of your work tasks? □

Add up your scores to measure your job satisfaction.

28–40 You seem highly motivated and fulfilled. However there is always scope for broadening your horizons and realising more of your potential.

16–27 You are only moderately fulfilled. Although parts of your work are satisfying, you are under-challenged and without some change in your current activities, you will feel bored and unfulfilled before long.

Under 16 You appear to receive minimal satisfaction from your work. Don't just accept this. Think about the options – developing your current role or an alternative, more satisfying, role.

Look back to the summary of your findings about yourself to see how your current job measures up to your profile.

What are your options?

♦ Improve your job satisfaction in your current job.

♦ Go for change or promotion in your organisation.

♦ Move to a different organisation.

♦ Change career direction.

♦ Choose a new way to work.

Improve your job satisfaction in your current job

If you feel that you don't want to move, or cannot, and there are no other opportunities that would suit you in your current organisation, then you will have to consider ways in which you could improve the quality of your current working experience for yourself. If you are discontented, don't think there is nothing to be done! Your interests are not best served by keeping a low profile and hoping for something better at a later date. There is no need simply to mark time in the job. The reasons for dissatisfaction are numerous and it is important to work out why you are feeling this way. Are you using your skills? Are your needs and values being met? Do you feel bored? Is your working environment getting you down? Are your work colleagues a source of irritation? Consider if you can do anything to put these problems right. One of the biggest causes of dissatisfaction at work is insufficient stimulus and challenge. You may feel, as a working mother, that you cannot take on any more stimulus and challenge – you have enough of that at home! You are tired out at the end of the day without adding to your 'to do' list. However, paradoxically, if you improve your job satisfaction by creating challenges for yourself, you will have *more* energy and feel *less* tired.

If you are fulfilled in your current job, the challenge is to build on the good work, discover and develop ways of moving forward, keeping a high profile and making the most of any opportunities that arise. This applies to part-time just as much as full-time work.

Improve your motivation

If you are bored, don't wait around to be offered opportunities to do things, volunteer. Look for areas where colleagues are under pressure and offer to lighten their workload. In this way you will get to know people doing a variety of jobs and, after experiencing your hard work and competence, they may be confident enough of your ability to give you more interesting and demanding tasks. You are then in a position to apply for those jobs where you have already gained some proficiency, when they become vacant.

Go on staff training courses such as skills training, assertiveness training, stress management or women into management.

Improve your working environment

♦ Suggest an improvement in the catering facilities, e.g. coffee machines, fridge, microwave, or new cups.

♦ Bring plants in to make the room more welcoming.

♦ Ask for an ioniser to be installed to improve the air quality.

♦ Campaign for new computers, photocopiers, washing facilities, telephone systems, better service contracts on equipment.

- Raise concerns about central heating, windows, lighting, furniture, general working conditions.

- Make better use of existing resources, e.g. training sessions for using present equipment and facilities.

Improve staff relationships

- Suggest team-building courses.

- Help to develop a friendlier atmosphere by celebrating staff birthdays and other special occasions.

- Ask for more support staff.

- Develop an induction scheme and a support system for new staff.

- Suggest regular meetings to discuss issues which arise.

- Ask for outside speakers to discuss sensitive issues.

Watch out for new initiatives in your organisation

- Job-sharing.

- Secondments to other parts of the organisation.

- Flexitime.

- Support for Open University courses.

- Career break schemes.

- Women-only courses.

- Crèche facilities.

Go for promotion in your organisation

Moving from your current place of work may be out of the question, but even if you are able to do so, it is always worth looking at the possibilities for change or promotion within your existing environment before considering moving. If you are keen to get promotion, it is important to understand the factors that determine whether or not people get promoted. A researcher identified three main factors in a number of organisations:

1 The quality of your work.

2 The image you create about yourself.

3 Whether people who are responsible for promotions in your organisation know about you.

The contributions of each of these factors to people being promoted were:

Work – 10%   Image – 30%   Visibility – 60%

This means that however good your work is, however indispensable you seem to be, you will not get promoted unless you are proactive in building your image and making sure you are known by the people who matter.

Dora's story

Dora had been working for the department for 20 years. She was everybody's friend. Nothing was too much trouble for her and she would help out when people were away, do photocopying for people who needed it 'urgently', and she was always rescuing people with computer problems and providing a listening ear for everyone's troubles. People would buy her a bottle of wine or flowers from time to time because she was so obliging. She was always in first in the morning, though she wasn't paid till 9am, but she needed the extra time to sort out everyone's mail and put the coffee on. Dora was a treasure. She helped all the new young people who wanted to know how things were organised and was happy when one of her trainees was promoted. Dora never got promoted because she was too useful where she was. She didn't understand why, since she worked so conscientiously and gave of her best at all times. She didn't realise she would never be considered for promotion if she made no effort to improve her image and build useful contacts.

Don't become a Dora doormat!

Get yourself noticed   If you want to be promoted, or to get yourself in a position where you are considered for promotion, you need to raise your professional profile so that more people know who you are and what you do. **How can you do this?**

Personal presentation   You can maximise the impact you have on other people by paying attention to your body language and your appearance, both of which are influenced by the feelings you have about yourself. Your body language can help you to look confident and receptive, or insecure and defensive. If you know yourself well and are clear about your strengths, then you have a good foundation for behaving in a confident way, walking tall, making eye contact easily, speaking clearly and audibly and having an open and friendly manner. If you do not feel you are demonstrating these qualities in your workplace, it is important to check what is going wrong and how you can learn to demonstrate more confident behaviour.

Pay attention to your posture, voice and eye contact. Good posture not only makes you look better, it can help you feel more energetic and on top of things.

Good eye contact is essential to demonstrate listening and giving attention to the speaker. It is particularly important to make good eye contact when you first speak to people and then look at them frequently when you talk. People who are embarrassed and feeling inferior demonstrate this immediately by looking away or giving short, infrequent glances. When talking to more than one person, you can demonstrate your confidence by sharing eye contact with everyone.

A controlled and confident voice is a valuable asset in getting yourself noticed. When other people feel comfortable with how you sound they will listen far more attentively to what you have to say. You can develop control over the volume and pitch of your voice by:

♦ Making sure you spend a few minutes each day practising deep breathing.

♦ Calming yourself when you feel nervous or under pressure, by taking a few slow controlled breaths *out* rather than concentrating on taking as much air *in* as possible.

We tend to think people with clear, audible voices are confident. If the voice is hesitant or mumbled we tend to attribute similar qualities to the person. It is worth working on projection and clarity by:

♦ Learning to relax your speech organs (jaw, tongue, lips and teeth) by releasing your jaw and yawning, chewing rapidly and stretching your lips backwards and forwards.

♦ Observing the effect on others when you are talking. Do you command more attention when you speak louder, more quietly, quicker or slower?

♦ Asking for feedback from other people and acting on the feedback received.

Your appearance Most of your body is covered by clothes at work, so you cannot ignore the messages that they give. If you give out a message that you do not care about yourself by wearing frumpy clothes, clashing colours or scuffed shoes, then it is likely that other people will feel the same way about you. If you dress well this gives a message that you care about yourself and your contribution to the workplace. This has a knock-on effect of making people feel secure, safe and confident in you. It influences the amount of attention you receive, the respect you are given and whether your other qualities are noticed. A professional image is not achieved by being in the height of fashion, or by dressing expensively, but by choosing the right clothes for your job and wearing them with style and confidence. Go for quality first and remember that your accessories, bag, briefcase, jewellery, pens, hairstyle, make-up, nails and so on, are an important part of the picture. Try to create a look that is an extension of your personality.

Assess how much your appearance is helping you raise your career profile by ticking the appropriate column in this chart for rating your self-presentation.

Your image		Letting me down	Can be a problem	Neutral influence	A plus for me	Spot on
Grooming	**make-up** *(have you altered this in the last few years?)*					
	hair *(style, colour)*					
	nails *(clean, filed, varnished?)*					
Clothes *(think about the style, age and quality of your clothes; do you wash and dry clean them regularly?)*	**shoes**					
	sweater					
	skirt					
	blouse					
	trousers					
	coat					
	jacket					
	tights/ stockings *(are they free of snags?)*					
Accessories	**briefcase** *(style, age)*					
	glasses *(style, age)*					
	belt					
	watch *(is it distinctive?)*					
	handbag					
Jewellery	**earrings**					
	bracelet					
	necklace					
	rings *(other than wedding and engagement)*					
	brooch					

Develop a specialism

Seek training and learning to increase your ability and specialist knowledge. Don't be put off if your organisation declines to pay for you; take responsibility for your own learning. You will impress those in authority with your determination. Find an area that interests you that is specialised and will get you noticed. You may be a whizz-kid on the computer or a creative writer. Whatever field you work in, be it IT, personnel, accountancy, social work or catering, there is always a possibility to develop some area of expertise in your job.

Develop a relationship with a mentor

Some organisations have formal mentoring schemes but if this is not offered at your place of work it is well worth approaching someone whom you like and respect to act as your mentor. It is important to choose a person who is going to be useful in helping you to further your career, though not usually someone with whom you have a supervisory connection. A mentor is generally someone older, more powerful and more experienced than you who serves as a guide, offering information, impartial advice and support. They need to be perceptive, a good listener, able to keep confidences and, above all, be interested in you and your progress. A good relationship with a mentor will be a considerable help to you in getting noticed. Mentors are usually in a position of authority with a wide variety of contacts and can speak for you in influential places; they may act as referees for you; they may decide, if they are successful, to offer you work when they are promoted. Finding someone like this is not easy and you may have to rely on more than one mentor who can offer you different things. For example, you may have recently come into a department from which a more senior colleague has transferred. She may be an invaluable help in telling you who and what to avoid, and how to deal with the day-to-day concerns. A person working for a similar organisation with whom you can discuss concerns and ways forward, may have broader and different experiences and offer new perspectives on the situation. It is down to you to search for willing mentors and one of the most likely sources is through your network of contacts. Don't give up if you cannot immediately identify anyone you could ask. Keep your eyes open. Develop and expand your network of contacts and you will eventually find someone whom you respect, trust and feel comfortable enough with to ask to be your mentor. Don't be shy – the person concerned will probably be flattered.

Talk about your work and goals

It is essential to let people know about your work and achievements. People are not mind-readers and if you do not tell them about your ideas, accomplishments and aspirations, no one else will. Make a feature of one of your achievements. Identify a successful project and offer to give a presentation about it at a meeting or write about it for the company newsletter. So many good women are overlooked for promotion because their image does not support and reinforce their talents. Check in the questionnaire that follows how people gain information about you at work.

How do you get your message across to people who are influential?

Think about the answers to these statements:

♦ People know I am doing my work well by ....

♦ People know I have the ability and experience to take on more responsibility by ....

♦ People know I would like more training by ....

♦ People know I am wanting change/promotion by ....

♦ People know I've improved my current skills and updated my knowledge by ....

♦ People know I enjoy my work by ....

♦ People know when I have a good idea for projects, training, new ways of working by ....

♦ People know what my goals are by ....

Make sure that you project an image that is true, does you justice and fits in with your goals. Find as many opportunities as you can to promote yourself. Socialise, network, mix with as many people as possible. Disclose your successes (learn to boast modestly!), verbally, or by memo if appropriate. Put real effort into presentations and written documents that may influence other people's views of your ability. Don't spend time dealing with trivia, or parts of your job that no-one else would know about; pick out the important and relevant parts of the work. Make sure your boss knows your aspirations.

Become more assertive at meetings

You may feel more nervous and threatened in meetings than in a one-to-one interaction and find difficulty in behaving assertively. A crucial first step is to ban yourself from using negative self-talk, e.g. *'I'm going to be ignored if I make any suggestions; being a woman in these situations is a real disadvantage,'* or *'If I don't understand something I daren't ask because they'll think, she's not up to this, and become irritated,'* and to substitute this for positive self-talk, .e.g. *'There may be prejudices around, but I can say clearly and concisely what I think,'* or *'I have the right to an explanation: I cannot contribute well in meetings if I haven't understood. It doesn't mean I'm not up to it.'*

When speaking in a meeting:

♦ Speak more loudly; raising your voice without raising the tone will help you to get into the discussion at the beginning and to prevent other people interrupting.

♦ Use 'I' statements to distinguish opinion from fact. *'As I see it ...'*, *'I believe we need to ...'*.

- Keep eye contact with all relevant group members. Try to ensure your eyes are directed at someone all the time, not just the chairperson. Avoid looking down at notes.

- If you are interrupted, say, *'I'd just like to finish what I'm saying.'*

- Don't fidget.

- Ask for reactions. *'What is your view?' 'What do you think of the idea?'*

When listening in a meeting:

- Don't look bored, doodle or surreptitiously read other material not relevant to the meeting. Don't have private conversations with others.

- Don't interrupt before someone else has finished (unless he or she has taken something you said the wrong way).

- If you want to disagree, do so assertively and constructively: *'I agree with the overall suggestion, but I don't agree that ...'*

- Ask assertively if you don't understand: *'Please could you clarify that point, Anne?' 'When you are talking about the budget are you talking about the total amount?'*

- Don't preface your comment with *'I think I'm being a bit dense about this ...'*

- If you agree, don't just nod your head, murmur *'yes, yes'* or smile supportively. Make sure you give verbal support. *'I agree with the suggestion, I think it will help us work as a team and keep us on track.'*

Contribute assertively to the running of meetings

Working mothers need to be assertive about the scheduling and organising of meetings. Meetings that are rescheduled, over-run, or held in a different location, can cause insuperable difficulty, so it is important to try to get agreement about keeping to dates, times and location of meetings whenever possible. It may help you to organise your time more easily if you are able to have, in advance, the minutes, agenda, expected length and other information about the meeting, so that you can you arrange to attend only the relevant parts; (you may be in a position to ask for a reorganising of the agenda).

Apply for a job in a different organisation

If you decide there is no scope for developing your current role where you are working at present, you may want to look for openings in other organisations. Don't be put off applying for jobs because you do not fit all the criteria specified in the job advert. Research studies of male and female applicants for jobs in a variety of fields show a striking difference in their confidence about their suitability for the job. Men see one of the requirements specified in a job description that fits in with their experience and skills and decide they fit the bill, whereas women see one which doesn't and don't apply! Although it would be nonsense to say this was true in all situations, it is an important to remind yourself that you will not get anywhere if you don't have a go.

Prepare yourself well

♦ Do your homework on the organisation; get as much information about the business as possible, from anyone you know who works there, from the press, from annual reports, company newsletters and so on.

♦ Read the relevant trade/industry magazine and become familiar with topical issues.

♦ Put real effort into your application form and curriculum vitae. Tailor each one specifically to the job you are applying for. Think of your CV as a Skills Profile and make it more individual by the use of headings which draw immediate attention to the fact that your skills and aptitudes match the employer's needs. Buy one of the excellent books on the market that give detailed information about preparing and writing applications and CVs.

♦ Prepare well for interviews. Check what you have written on your application form, make a note of what you think they are looking for, what you can offer them, and have a clear idea of the main points you want to get across. When you are happy with what you want to say, role-play the interview with a friend. Make the interview as authentic as you can; put on the clothes you have chosen to wear on the day, make sure you are left undisturbed, and position your chair appropriately. Practise boasting modestly, answering difficult questions, pacing your answers and above all being enthusiastic. Ask for feedback on how you come across. Having your ideas clear and practising before the interview in this way helps to steady your nerves on the day.

Make speculative applications

About two-thirds of all jobs are never advertised, so it is important to consider ways of promoting yourself to those companies that are likely to find you a suitable employee. This kind of application needs careful research and preparation. Focus on one company and find out exactly what they do. Make sure you have thought about what you have to offer and how this fits in with the needs of this target company. Always keep your focus on what they need, not what you want. You may decide to telephone, or write to the company, even though no vacancy has been advertised. The obvious person to target is the Personnel Officer or the individual who deals with recruitment. Make sure you have the spelling and the gender right. Explain what you have to offer, ask for a meeting if at all possible and for your details to be kept on file.

Network Make sure as many people as possible are aware of your career plans. Renew old contacts, use friends, people working in target companies, other women's networks in your profession, area or industry, to find out about job opportunities and spread the word. Voluntary work, temporary jobs, community work, evening classes, can all help to extend your personal network. Make it routine to ask each of your contacts for the name of another person they know who may be able to help you in your chosen field. It is often an introduction to a friend of a friend which eventually leads to a job. One of the benefits of belonging to a network, whether through a formal or informal group, is that it enables you to meet other people, exchange ideas, and feel less isolated in the pursuit of your goal.

Change career direction

Do you feel you have reached a cross-roads in your career or your life, and want to change direction? The fact that you have recognised this is an important first step. So many of us put off making decisions until ... Christmas is over, mother-in-law leaves, the baby goes to playgroup, the children go to secondary school, our divorce comes through, or whatever else persuades us that now isn't the right time. Career experts are forecasting that employees working over the next 20 years will have to retrain three or four times in the course of their careers. Keywords for the next decade are competition, flexibility and survival.

Where do you start? You need to be fully aware of your abilities and aptitudes. If you are not, it is difficult to convince a prospective employer that you can do something different from the jobs you have done so far in your career. Use the information you have collected about yourself earlier in the book as a basis for action. Supplement this groundwork with further self-development work. Visit your local library, careers office, or adult education advisor for advice on further reading, contacts and trade associations to research options.

If you decide on a new career direction, make sure you gain some insight into the area of work and the work content of specific jobs in the field. You may have wanted to be a primary school teacher for as long as you can remember but unless you have a thorough knowledge of the day-to-day work by being in the classroom before you take the plunge and start training, you will not be sure it's right for you. Ask people you know who work in the field whether you could spend some time shadowing them. Careers officers from your local careers service may be able to help (this service is not just for school leavers and students). The time you need to spend 'work shadowing' may have to be taken from your annual leave if you are working full-time. Volunteer work and charity work may provide you with opportunity to find out exactly what your chosen job involves. Offering to work for a company for nothing can give you not only experience but also a reference and, if you chose a well-known company, an impressive name on your CV. Of course it's all very well working for nothing but how are you supposed to survive while you do it? You need to consider the terms under which you are willing to work and remember you have something to offer. It is worth asking for some contribution to your travel and other expenses incurred through your working for them. Some working mothers in our survey who couldn't find work after a career break, got their current jobs by working for a company without pay initially.

ill: '*The local radio station tried to put me off working for nothing by saying that I would only be answering the phone and making coffee, but after a week someone was ill and I was ringing up local newspapers and helping out with interviews. After a few weeks, I taped an interview with a local person that was really funny and they used it. I was thrilled. I was paid for freelance work for a while and after a year I was on a part-time contract.*'

Janet: '*I worked for a month part-time for a design company without pay to see what the work involved and when I left they asked me to stay in touch, which I did. They asked me to go back over the summer for two months paid work and then I was kept on permanently.*'

The implications of change If you want to make a big career change you'll most probably need qualifications. The Learning and Skills Council may be able to advise you. Retraining needs time and money. Before embarking on the change you will have to decide whether you are committed enough to spend the next two or three years poring over books. Will you be able to cope with your everyday family responsibilities without getting too stressed? How great a commitment will your retraining demand from others in the family? Are you willing to manage on less money for a while? Many women stay put because they can't afford to leave work and go into full-time training, though others prefer to live frugally for a while in exchange for the long-term financial benefits of a career change.

It is sensible to be realistic and take account of the ever-changing job market before deciding on your career change. You need to consider those job sectors where opportunities are on the increase, not on the decline. The likely growth areas for the next decade include:

♦ Information technology. This is well paid and can offer good promotion prospects. Research suggests that unless more women take up careers in IT, the industry faces a chronic skills shortage.

- Leisure/sports. Keeping fit is a boom industry. Masseuses, aromatherapists, sports therapists are in real demand.

- Public relations. There are more openings than ever; being a PR officer gives you a very varied career.

- Education and training. There are openings for career counsellors, personal counsellors, drama therapists, child welfare workers, educational psychologists, speech therapists as well as teachers for all age groups.

- Hotels and catering.

- Technical writing and translation.

- Voluntary bodies, charities.

- Paralegal. New and exciting opportunities are opening up in the legal world for those without a law degree.

If you are thinking about something unusual that offers a good chance of a job, consider the following: horticultural therapist, environmental impact consultant, paramedic, homeopath, priest, arts administrator, train driver, organic farmer, ergonomist, film liaison officer, European Union worker.

Choose a new way to work

You may feel that you want to change to a job that allows you more flexibility or shorter hours.

Job-sharing This involves two people sharing one full-time job between them including the pay, holidays and workload. One advantage of job-sharing is that you can apply for a position, with a colleague or friend, that would not normally be offered on a part-time basis. This might involve more responsibility, chance for promotion and a more attractive salary than the majority of part-time work available.

- You may need to find someone with similar skills, training and experience as yourself and together apply for a job which is advertised.

- You may like to consider whether your current job could be shared with another person, allowing you to take on different responsibilities for the other half of your job, or to work part-time. This may be a real possibility for you if you have been with your organisation for several years and you are considered an invaluable employee.

- Apply to employment agencies with a partner to see if they can find you work together. You may also discuss the possibility of being put in touch with others in your position.

Jane's story

When my children were young, I saw a teaching post advertised for a local school that I really fancied. I persuaded a friend in a similar situation to apply with me. We considered all the objections that might be raised against job-sharing and rehearsed our answers thoroughly. At the interview we were really enthusiastic and convinced everyone we could do just as good a job as a single teacher, if not better.

We were given the position, which we have now held for five years. We are both happy with the arrangement and even if one of us should decide to leave, I don't see any problem with finding a replacement.

Temporary work Do you have a skill to offer such as word-processing, teaching or nursing skills, which would give you the option of choosing temporary employment? The main advantages are being able to choose when you work, avoiding such times as school holidays, the variety of work and workplaces you experience, and the different people you meet. On the down side, the wages are usually lower, you have no guarantee of work and you don't get any of the perks such as holiday pay or sick pay with most agencies.

Work for yourself The idea of working for yourself, particularly if you have young children, may seem an ideal solution. The points below may be seen by you as advantages of self-employment. Tick any of them that appeal to you.

◆ I could work the hours I wanted to and stop when I liked.

◆ There would be far less difficulty for me if the children were ill.

◆ I could save money on childcare.

◆ I would be able to make money out of one of my interests or an idea I have had.

◆ I would avoid the daily grind of travel and the difficult relationships at work.

◆ I would spend my time doing things I chose to do.

◆ I could make more money than I get now if I were successful.

◆ I could organise my life better and spend more time with my family.

◆ I would become more confident.

◆ I would feel free and independent.

◆ I would earn the respect of my friends.

◆ I could involve my partner, family and friends more closely in my work.

- ♦ I would feel in control of my own work.

- ♦ I would not have the problem of facing redundancy.

- ♦ I would be more excited and enthusiastic about my work.

You may feel fired up and raring to go, but you do need to consider all the disadvantages as well. Setting up on your own can be a risky business especially if you have had no previous experience of working for yourself. The statistics are not very encouraging. Three out of four businesses will survive their first year, but only one out of five will survive for five years, if recent trends continue.

Read through the points below, which you might consider as disadvantages of self - employment, and put a cross by any that seem unattractive to you.

- ♦ I would have to learn about business management which may entail evening classes.

- ♦ I would have to be responsible for the financial and legal aspects of the work.

- ♦ I may have to borrow money or use my savings.

- ♦ I may have to work while children are demanding attention.

- ♦ I may have to give up my current job.

- ♦ I may miss the company of colleagues.

- ♦ I may have to market products and sell things.

- ♦ I would have to make business plans and keep records.

- ♦ I may have to be away from home more often.

- ♦ I may have to work much harder, including weekends and evenings.

- ♦ I may have less time for socialising with friends and family.

- ♦ I may have to live with less money, or lose money.

- ♦ I may have to involve other people in helping me.

- ♦ I may have to develop more assertive skills.

- ♦ I would have to be more organised.

- ♦ I would have to arrange my own taxes, insurance, holiday pay, money to cover days off sick.

If you have ticked many items in the first list and crossed few in the second list you are the type of person to be attracted to working for yourself. The range of self-employed work that you can consider is huge. You may have a particular skill such as computing, cooking, or writing; you may offer a service such as babyminding, driving or gardening or be able to provide in-service training for schools, or conference-organising for companies. You may have an idea for a business that has arisen out of a hobby or interest. If you do consider setting up on your own, the most important first step is to seek advice to find out whether your idea is a good one and is financially viable, and to gain some insight into all that is entailed in setting up on your own. Advice is readily and freely available from banks, job centres, careers services and the government's agency Business Link, which acts as a one stop shop for new businesses, running start-up training courses and advising on grants available. You should also investigate open learning schemes provided by organisations like the Open College and the Industrial Society, which runs courses for potential entrepreneurs. Your local authority will be keen to encourage your efforts and will be able to give you helpful advice as to what is available in your own area.

If you do establish that there is a market for your goods or service, you have sufficient capital to start off, you know how to promote yourself effectively, manage your time efficiently and are realistic in your expectations of what you can achieve at first, then you are ready to go.

Your work is very likely to involve working from home initially. You will need:

♦ Some uninterrupted time. This means childcare may need to be organised.

♦ Dedicated space which, if possible, is out of bounds to the children.

♦ A separate telephone with an answering machine (essential if the children are at home whilst you are working).

♦ The self-discipline to work your planned number of hours each day and shut your eyes and ears to housework and interruptions.(Keep a kettle in your workroom to save you having to go to the kitchen.)

♦ Clear rules about not being disturbed that have been discussed with friends, neighbours and family.

♦ A professional attitude to your work. (Some mothers working from home say it helps them feel more professional if they dress for work and get changed at the end of their working day.)

Programme Review

Now that you have reached the end of this self-help book and looked at the various aspects of your roles as a worker and mother, you will have discovered and practised positive ways for coping with these dual roles. Think back through the topics you have covered and, using the information and insight you have gained, mark the appropriate column in the boxes below to determine where you will need to take action.

	I am happy with this	I need to work on this
You		
I am now aware of the range of pressures that affect my life		
I understand the influences that affect my ideal self		
I can now reconcile my actual self with my ideal self		
I can now deal with negative views and feelings that are bound to affect me at times and that may influence my behaviour		
I understand the impact of guilt on my view of myself and my relationships with others		
I can deal with the resentment and anger that I feel		
I can now cope more positively with stress and take care of myself		
I have learned how I can make changes in my life		
I can now see a way forward for striking a healthier balance between work and home		

	I am happy with this	I need to work on this
You and your child		
I understand how my own upbringing influences my relationship with my child		
I can see which aspects of the relationship with my child are causing me concern		
I can now develop better communication skills with my child		
I can now encourage my child's cooperation		
I can now encourage my child's independence		
You and your work		
I understand how being a mother affects my work		
I am aware of the time and energy I want to give to my professional development		
I am aware of the skills I have and how these could be developed further		
I am aware of my personality characteristics and work values		
I am aware of what is stopping me from developing my career		
I am aware of my career options		
I can see how I could improve my interest and satisfaction in my current job		
I understand how I could change career direction		

Training and Resources

Training

If you have enjoyed this book and think that your employer or other organisation would like to host a personal development course, you may like further details of our training.

The guidance and exercises in our books are brought powerfully to life in our one-day or two-day **Boost Your Energy, Personal Power** and **She Who Dares Wins** courses.

Explore personal effectiveness safely within a lively programme, expertly facilitated by one of our trainers. Our team consistently receive high scores in post-course feedback and are known for their warm, practical approach spiced with honesty and humour.

Participants are led gently through self-awareness exploration and are inspired to try new effective approaches, making clear action plans for the future and taking away a range of practical techniques for a more empowered future.

For more information on these and other courses for adults, or to have an informal discussion, contact our Project Manager by one of the means listed overleaf.

Books

Two further publications by Jenny Mosley and Eileen Gillibrand are available and can be ordered by post or via our website.

♦ **Personal Power: how to fulfil your private and professional life**
Forerunner to *She Who Dares Wins*, featuring a shorter version of the workbook but still packed with self-assessment exercises about assertiveness, handling stress, time management and more. Aimed originally at women it can be just as valuable for men. A book that is low on 'waffle' and high on information and action.

♦ **She Who Dares Wins: a woman's guide to professional and personal success**
An extended version of the Personal Power workbook, taking the four themes of self-esteem, stress, assertiveness and management skills and developing them further. In addition to the self-assessment exercises, clear diagrams and examples concisely capture the learning points for you to consider before setting goals and practising the techniques to fulfil your potential.

Resources for schools

Additionally, Jenny Mosley and her team offer an extensive range of self-esteem based courses, publications and products specifically designed for schools, based on her **Whole School Quality Circle Time Model** which has revolutionised the approach to self-esteem and behaviour management at all ages. With increasing interest internationally, Quality Circle Time has been rapidly growing in use in the UK since 1980 and is recognised by educational leaders as a very effective way forward in schools. See our latest catalogue for full details.

Contact details

To order books, request a catalogue or obtain further information on training courses including a list of accredited trainers, please contact us in any of the following ways. We look forward to hearing from you.

Training and general enquiries: tel. 01225 767157   Fax 01225 755631
Books and products: tel. 01225 719204   Fax 01225 712187
E-mail: circletime@jennymosley.demon.co.uk
Website: www. jennymosley.demon.co.uk

Jenny Mosley Consultancies / Positive Press Ltd
28A Gloucester Road
Trowbridge
Wiltshire
BA14 0AA
England